THE MOST REQUESTED

Songs of t s

Cherry Lane Music Company
Director of Publications/Project Editor: Mark Phillips

ISBN 978-1-4768-7429-6

CONTENTS

$2

Along Comes Mary

Words and Music by
Tandyn Almer

D/A Am7 D/A
in rhyme and verse and curse those faults in me. And then a-
make jokes at who is most to blame to-day. And then a-
are left un-sung and hung up-on the scars. And then a-
E A E7 A E A
long comes Mar-y. And does she want to give me kicks, and be my stead-y
long comes Mar-y. And does she want to set them free, and let them see re-
long comes Mar-y. And does she want to see the stains, the dead re-mains of
E7 A E A D G
chick and give me pick of mem-o-ries?
al-i-ty from where she got her name?
all the pains she left the night be-fore?
B E B E B E
Or may-be rath-er gath-er tales of all the fails and trib-u-la-tions no one ev-er
Then will they strug-gle much when told that such a ten-der touch as hers will make them not the
Or will their wak-ing eyes re-flect the lies, and make them re-a-lize their ur-gent cry for

F#m/A
Bm7/A
A7
Dm
Em7
F
sees.
same?
sight no more?
When we met I was sure out to
To Coda
Dm
D
Am
B/A
lunch. Now my emp - ty cup tastes as sweet as the punch.
Am7
Bm/A
1
When vague de -
2
Am
D

Am
Bm/A
Am
Bm/A
D.S. al Coda
And when the
CODA
Am
Bm7
Sweet as the
Am
B/A
Am
B/A
punch.
Sweet as the punch.
Am
Bm/A
Am
Sweet as the punch.
Sweet as the punch.

And I Love Her

Words and Music by
John Lennon and Paul McCartney

F♯m
C♯m
4fr
A
And if you saw my love you'd love her too.
The kiss my lov - er brings she brings to me.
I know this love of mine will nev - er die.
B
E6
To Coda
1
I love her.
And I love her.
And I love her.
2
C♯m
4fr
B
A love like ours
C♯m
4fr
G♯m
4fr
C♯m
4fr
could nev - er die as long as I

G♯m
4fr
B
D.S. al Coda
have you near me.
CODA
Gm
3fr
Instrumental solo
Bright are the stars
Dm
Gm
3fr
Dm
that shine,
dark is the sky.
Gm
3fr
Dm
B♭
I know this love of mine
will nev - er die.

C
1
F6
End instrumental solo
And I love
2
F6
her.
Gm
3fr
F6
Gm
3fr
D

Apples, Peaches, Pumpkin Pie

Words and Music by
Maurice Irby, Jr.

Additional Lyrics

2. Apples, peaches, pumpkin pie,
You were young and so was I.
Now that we've grown up it seems
You just keep ignorin' me.
I'll find you anywhere you go,
I'm gonna look high and low.
You can't escape this love of mine anytime.
Well, I'll sneak up behind you,
Be careful where I find you.

3. Apples, peaches, pumpkin pie,
Soon your love will be all mine.
Then I'm gonna take you home,
Marry you so you won't roam.
I'll find you anywhere you go,
I'm gonna look high and low.
You can't escape this love of mine anytime.
Well, I'll sneak up behind you,
Be careful where I find you.

Aquarius

from the Broadway Musical Production HAIR

Words by
James Rado and Gerome Ragni

Music by Galt MacDermot

Dm
G7
Am
peace will guide the plan - ets,
and love will steer the
F
G7
C
N.C.
B♭
stars. This is the dawn - ing of the age of A -
quar - i - us, the age of A - quar - i - us.

Dm
G7
A - quar - i - us,
A -
Dm
Fine
quar - i - us.
C7
F
C7
F
Har-mo-ny and un-der-stand - ing,
sym-pa-thy and trust a-bound - ing.

C7
F
C7
F
No more false-hoods or de - ri - sions, gold - en liv - ing dreams of vi - sions, mys - tic
A7/E
Dm
Gm
Am
crys - tal rev - e - la - tion, and the mind's true lib - er - a - tion. A -
Gm
quar - i - us,
A -
Dm
D.S. al Fine
quar - i - us.
When the

Are You Lonesome Tonight?

Words and Music by
Roy Turk and Lou Handman

C F Fm C C7 F
heart? Do the chairs in your par - lor seem emp - ty and
Cm 3fr D7 G7 F#7 G7
bare? Do you gaze at your door - step and pic - ture me there? Is your
C C7 C#dim7 D7 G7
heart filled with pain, shall I come back a - gain? Tell me, dear, are you
1 C D7♭9 4fr G7
2 C F Fm C
lone - some to - night? Are you night?
rit.

The Beat Goes On

Words and Music by
Sonny Bono

Char - les - ton was once the rage, uh - huh.
gro - c'ry store does su - per - mart, uh - huh.
Grand - mas sit in chairs and rem - i - nisce.
His - to - ry has turned a page, uh - huh. The
Lit - tle girls still break their hearts, uh - huh. And
Boys keep chas - ing girls to get a kiss. The
min - i - skirt's the cur - rent thing, uh - huh.
men still keep on march - ing off to war.
cars keep go - ing fast - er all the time.
Last time D.S. and Fade
Teen - y bop - per is our new - born king, uh - huh.
'Lec - tric - 'ly they keep their base - ball score.
Bums still cry, "Hey bud - dy, have you got a dime?"
And the beat goes on,

Beyond the Sea

Lyrics by Jack Lawrence

Music by
Charles Trenet and Albert Lasry
Original French Lyric to "La Mer" by Charles Trenet

F/A Dm B♭ D7/A Gm C7 C♯dim
3fr
4fr
stands on gold - en sands and watch - es the
flets d'ar - gent la mer, Des re - flets change -
Dm B♭ G7 C C7/B♭ F Dm
5fr
ships that go sail - ing. Some - where
ants sous la plu - ie. La mer
B♭ C7 F Dm B♭ C7
be - yond the sea, he's (she's) there watch - ing for
au ciel d'é - té Con - fond ses blancs mou -
F A7/E Dm C7 C7/B♭ F/A Dm B♭ D7/A
5fr
me. If I could fly like birds on high,
tons A - vec les anges si purs, la mer

Gm C7 C♯dim Dm B♭ Gm7 C7 F E7
3fr
4fr
then straight to his (her) arms I'd go sail - ing. It's
Ber - gér - e d'a - zur in - fi - ni - e Voy -
A F♯m7 D6 E7 A F♯m7
far be - yond a star; it's
ez près des é - tangs Ces
D6 E7 A A/G♯ A/F♯ A/E G7 C Am
near be - yond the moon. I know
grands ro - seaux moui - llés. Voy - ez
F G7 C Am F6 G7
be - yond a doubt, my heart will lead me there
ces oi - seaux blancs Et ces mai - sons roui -

C C/B♭ Am C7 F Dm B♭ C7
soon. We'll meet be - yond the
llées. La mer les a ber -
F Dm B♭ C7 F A7/E Dm C7 C7/B♭
5fr
shore; we'll kiss just as be - fore. Hap - py we'll
cés Le long des golf - es clairs Et d'une chan -
F/A Dm B♭ D7/A Gm C7 C♯dim Dm B♭
3fr
4fr
be be - yond the sea, and nev - er a - gain I'll go
son d'a mour, la mer A ber - cé mon coeur pour la
1
G7 C7 F Gm7 C7
sail - ing. Some -
vi - e. La
2
G7 C7 F
sail - ing.
vi - e.
3

Big Girls Don't Cry

Words and Music by
Bob Crewe and Bob Gaudio

A♭
F7
B♭m7
E♭7
A♭
F7
Big girls don't cry.
(Who said
B♭m7
E♭7
A♭
F7
B♭m7
E♭7
they don't cry?)
My girl said good - bye, my, oh my.
Ba - by, I was cruel, I was cruel.
A♭
F7
B♭m7
E♭7
A♭
F7
My girl
Ba - by,
B♭m7
E♭7
A♭
D♭
did - n't cry.
I'm a fool.
(I won - der
(I'm such a
4fr

A♭
A♭+
F7
why.) (Sil - ly boy.) Told my girl we
fool.) (Sil - ly girl.) Shame on you, your
B♭7
had to break up. (Sil - ly boy.) Thought that she would
ma - ma said. (Sil - ly girl.) Shame on you, you're
E♭7
call my bluff. (Sil - ly boy.) Then she said, to my sur - prise,
cry'n' in bed. (Sil - ly girl.) Shame on you, you told a lie.
A♭
Cm/E♭
D♭
E♭7
A♭
F7
"Big girls don't do cry." Big girls

Bbm7
Eb7
Ab
F7
Bbm7
Eb7
don't cry, they don't cry.
Ab
F7
Bbm7
Eb7
1 Ab
F7
Big girls don't cry.
(Who said
Bbm7
Eb7
2 Ab
F7
Bbm7
Eb7
they don't cry?) cry.
(That's just an al - i - bi.)
Ab
Cm/Eb
Db
Eb7
Ab
Cm/Eb
Db
Eb7
Big girls don't cry, big girls don't cry.

Build Me Up, Buttercup

Words and Music by
Tony McCauley and Michael D'Abo

F
G11
C
G7
say you will (say you will) but I love you still; I need you (I need you) more than an -
C7
F
Fm
E7♯5
Fm6
- y - one dar - ling you know that I have from the start. So
To Coda
C
G7
F
C
Dm7
C
build me up (build me up) but - ter-cup don't break my heart.
G
C
G
I'll be ov - er at ten, you tell me
To you I'm a toy but I could

B♭
F
C
time and a - gain but you're late,
be the boy you a - dore.
I wait a -
If you just
Dm
Dm9
3fr
G7
C
G
round and then:
let me know:
I run to the door, I can't take
and though you're un - true I'm at - tract -
B♭
F
C
an - y more, it's not you,
- ed to you all the more
you let me
why do I
Dm
C
Dm
Dm
G7
C
Dm
down a - gain.
need you so?
Ba - by ba - by
try to find

Em
A7
Dm
A7
Dm
a lit - tle time and I'll make you hap - py, I'll be home, I'll be be -
D7
G
side the phone wait - ing for you.
3
2nd time D.S. al Coda
Gsus
G13
G9sus
G13
G11
G9sus
G13
3fr
Oo
Oo
Why do you
f
CODA
F
C
Dm7
C
Don't break my heart.

California Sun

Words and Music by
Morris Levy and Henry Glover

C
F
C
walk and I walk, they twist and I'll
F
C
F
twist. They shim and I'll shim, they
C
F
C
B♭7
fly and I'll fly. Well, they're out there hav - ing
A7
D7
G7
1, 2
C
3
C
fun, in the warm Cal - i - for - nia sun.
I'm
The

Can't Help Falling in Love

from the Paramount Picture BLUE HAWAII

Words and Music by
George David Weiss, Hugo Peretti
and Luigi Creatore

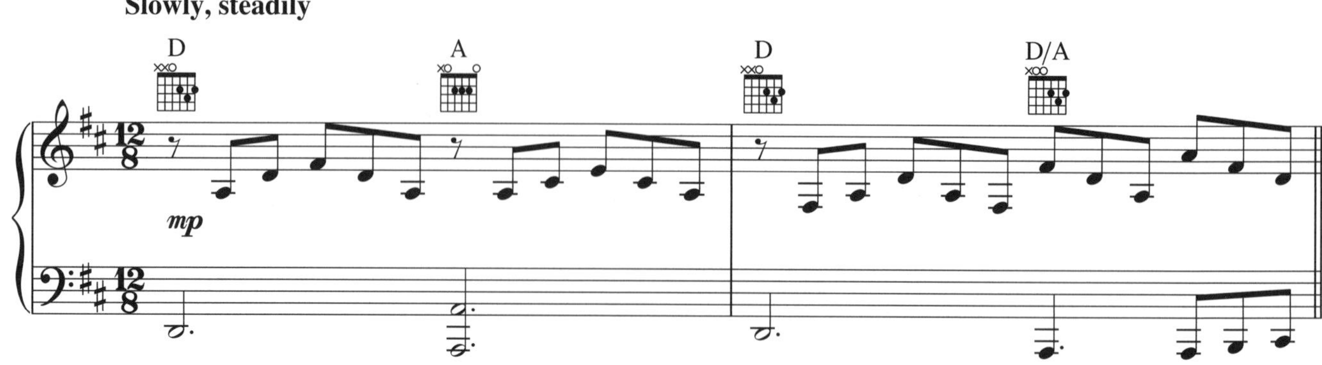

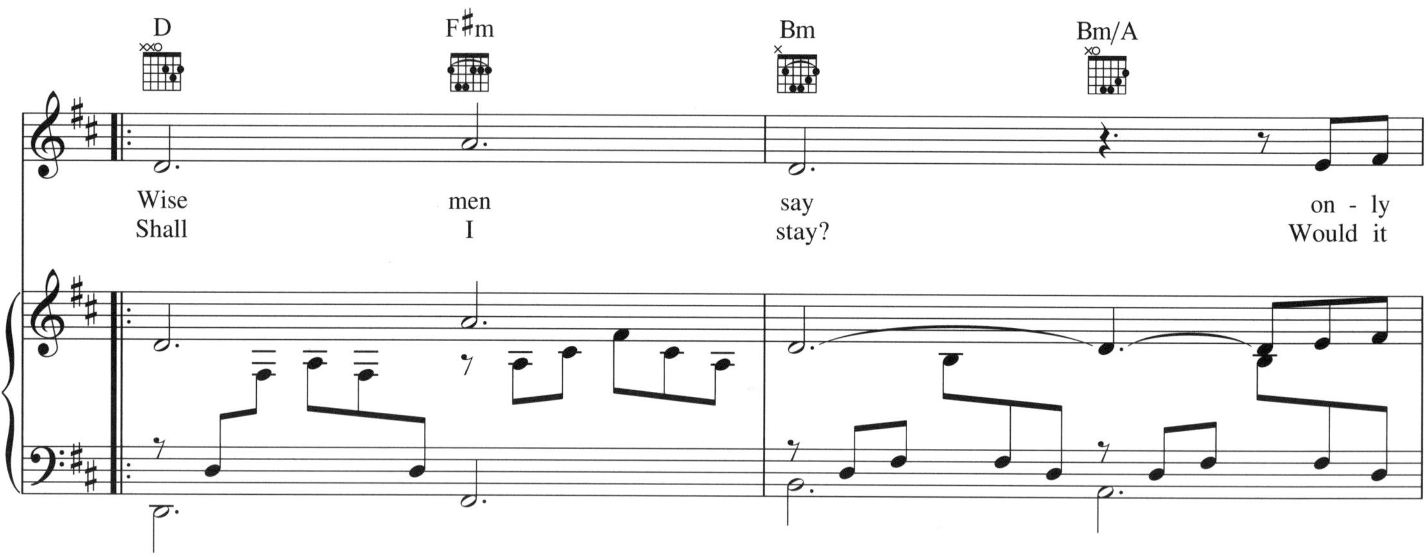

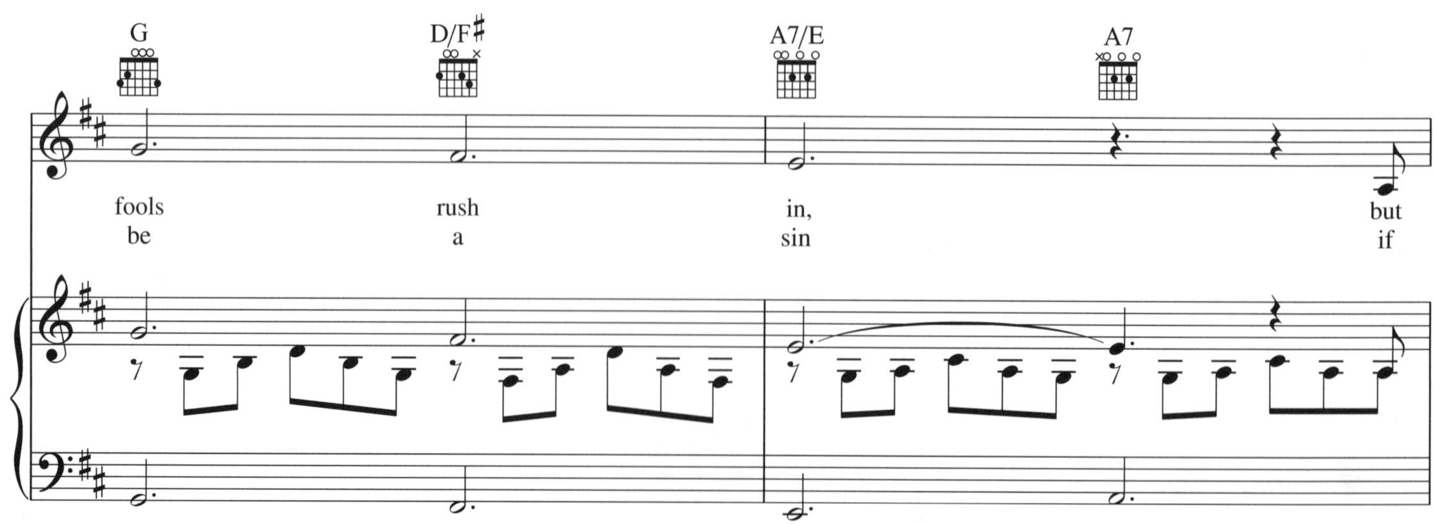

G
A
Bm
G6
Em
I can't help fall - ing in
I can't help fall - ing in
D/A
A7
1
D
D/A
love with you.
love with
2
D
F♯m
C♯
you?
Like a riv - er flows
F♯m
C♯
F♯m
C♯
sure - ly to the sea,
dar - ling, so it goes;

F♯m
B7
Em
A7
some things are meant to be.
D
F♯m
Bm
Take my hand, take my
G
D/F♯
A7/E
A7
whole life too, for
G
A
Bm
G6
Em
I can't help fall - ing in

1
2
D/A
A7
D
D/A
love
with
you.
D
G
A
you.
For
I
can't
Bm
G6
Em
D/A
A7
help
fall - ing in
love
with
rit.
D
you.

Can't Take My Eyes Off of You

Words and Music by
Bob Crewe and Bob Gaudio

A♭m
4fr
E♭
love has ar-rived, and I thank God I'm a-live.
feel like I feel, please let me know that it's real.
You're just too
F7
A♭m6
1
E♭
good to be true, can't take my eyes off of you.
Par-don the
2
E♭
Fm7♭5
Fm7
A♭m/B♭
Fm7/B♭
eyes off of you.
E♭+
E♭6

To Coda
Eb+
Eb6
Eb+
Eb6
C7#9
Fm7
I love you, ba - by, and if it's
Bb7
Eb
Cm7
3fr
quite all right, I need you, ba - by, to warm the lone - ly night. I love you,
Fm7
Fm7/Bb
Bb7
Eb6
ba - by, trust in me when I say:
Cm7
3fr
Fm7
Bb7
Oh, pret - ty ba - by, don't bring me down, I pray. Oh, pret - ty

E♭
Cm7
Fm7
ba - by, now that I've found you, stay, and let me love you, ba - by. Let me
D♭9
D♭7
B♭7
D.S. al Coda
(with repeat)
CODA
love you. You're just too
ba - by, and if it's
B♭7
E♭
Cm7
quite all right, I need you, ba - by, to warm the lone - ly night. I love you,
Fm7
B♭7
E♭6
Cm7
Repeat and Fade
ba - by, trust in me when I say:
Oh, pret - ty

Can't You Hear My Heart Beat

Words and Music by
John Carter and Ken Lewis

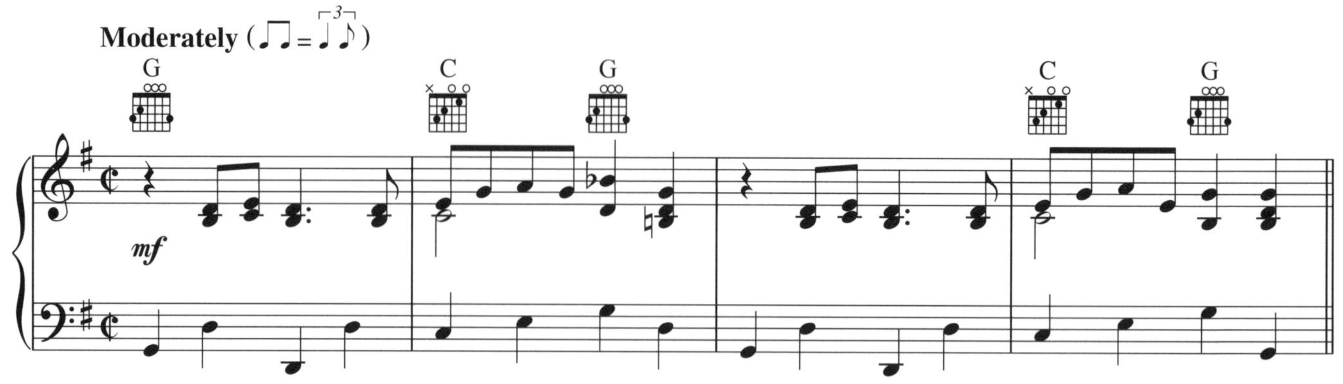

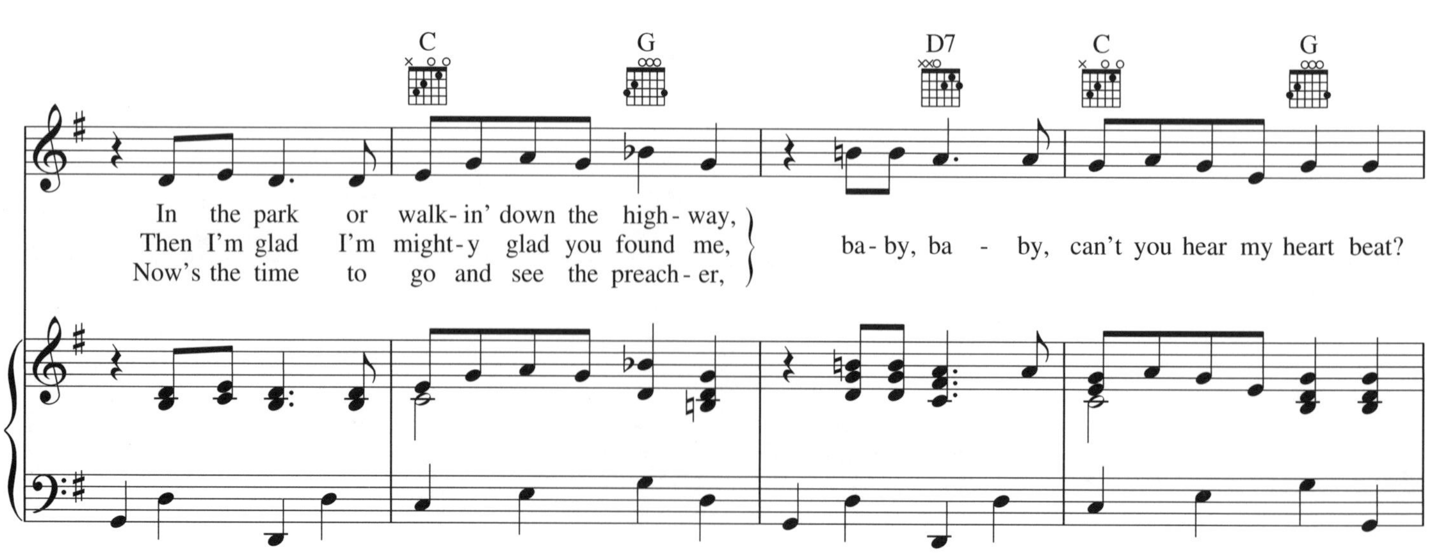

C
D
When you move up clos-er to me, I get a feel-ing that's oo ee, yeah.
When you asked me to meet your ma, I know that, ba - by, we'd be go-ing far, yeah.
Wed-ding bells are go-ing to chime, and ba - by, ba - by, you're gon-na be mine, yeah.
G
C
G
C
G
D7
Can't you hear the pound-in' of my heart beat? You're the one I love.
1, 2
3
You're the one I love.
You're the one I love.
You're the one I love.
You're the one I love.

Chapel of Love

Words and Music by
Phil Spector, Ellie Greenwich
and Jeff Barry

Gm
C7
F
go - in' to the chap - el of love.
Gm7
F
Gm7
F
C7
F
Spring is here, the
Bells will ring, the
C7
F
Gm
sky is blue, whoa, birds will
sun will shine, whoa, I'll be
C7
Gm
C7
sing as if they knew.
his and he'll be mine.

F
C7
F
Cm6
3fr
D7
To - day's the day
we'll say, "I do."
We'll love un - til
the end of time.
And we'll
Gm
3fr
C7
1
F
C7
nev - er be lone - ly an - y - more.
Be - cause we're
2
F
C7
D.S. al Coda
CODA
Gm
3fr
more.
Be - cause we're
go - in'
Go - in'
to the
Repeat and Fade
Optional Ending
C7
F
Gm7
F
Gm7
F
chap - el of love.

Cherish

Words and Music by
Terry Kirkman

Bb
Am
told you. You don't know how man - y times I've wished that I could
dreams. That I am not gon - na be the one to share your
Bb
Am
hold you. You don't know how man - y times I've wished that I could
schemes. That I am not gon - na be the one to share what
To Coda
Bb
Am
Gm
3fr
Bb
mold you in - to some - one who could cher - ish me as much as I cher - ish
seems to be the life that you could cher - ish as much as I do
1
C
2
C
you.
yours. Oh, I'm be -

Gm
C
Am
gin - ning to think that man has nev - er found the words that could make you want
E
C
F
Dm7
me. That have the right a - mount of let - ters, just the right sound, that could
B♭
Gm
E♭
make you hear, make you see that you are driv - ing me out of my
C
N.C.
F
mind. Oh, I could say I need you, but then you'd

C/E
Cm/E♭
D7
re - al - ize that I want you, just like a thou-sand oth - er guys who'd say they
B♭
C7
Dm
B♭
loved you with all the rest of their lies, when all they want-ed was to touch your face, your
Gm7
E♭6
C
D.S. al Coda
hands, and gaze in - to your eyes.
CODA
E♭
cher - ish me as much as I cher - ish

C
F
B♭
C
you.
And I do
F
B♭
C
cher - ish you.
And I
C
F
B♭
C
do
cher - ish you.
F6/9
Cher - ish is the word.
rit.

Crimson and Clover

Words and Music by
Tommy James and Peter Lucia

G
C
G
F
now when she comes walk - ing o - ver,
now I've been wait - ing to show her
crim - son and clo - ver,
o - ver and o - ver.
(♩ = 𝅗𝅥)

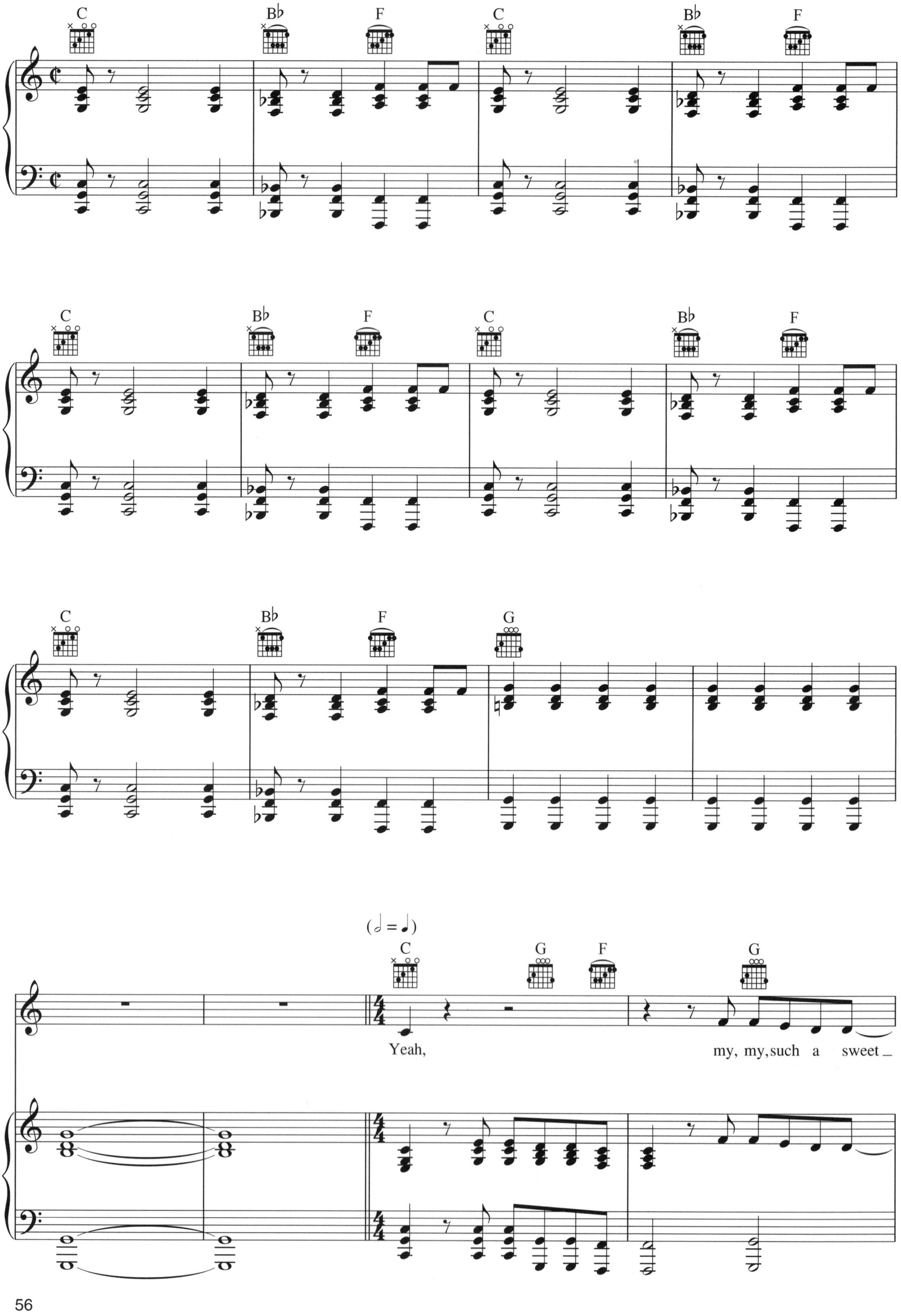

C Bb F C Bb F

C Bb F C Bb F

C Bb F G

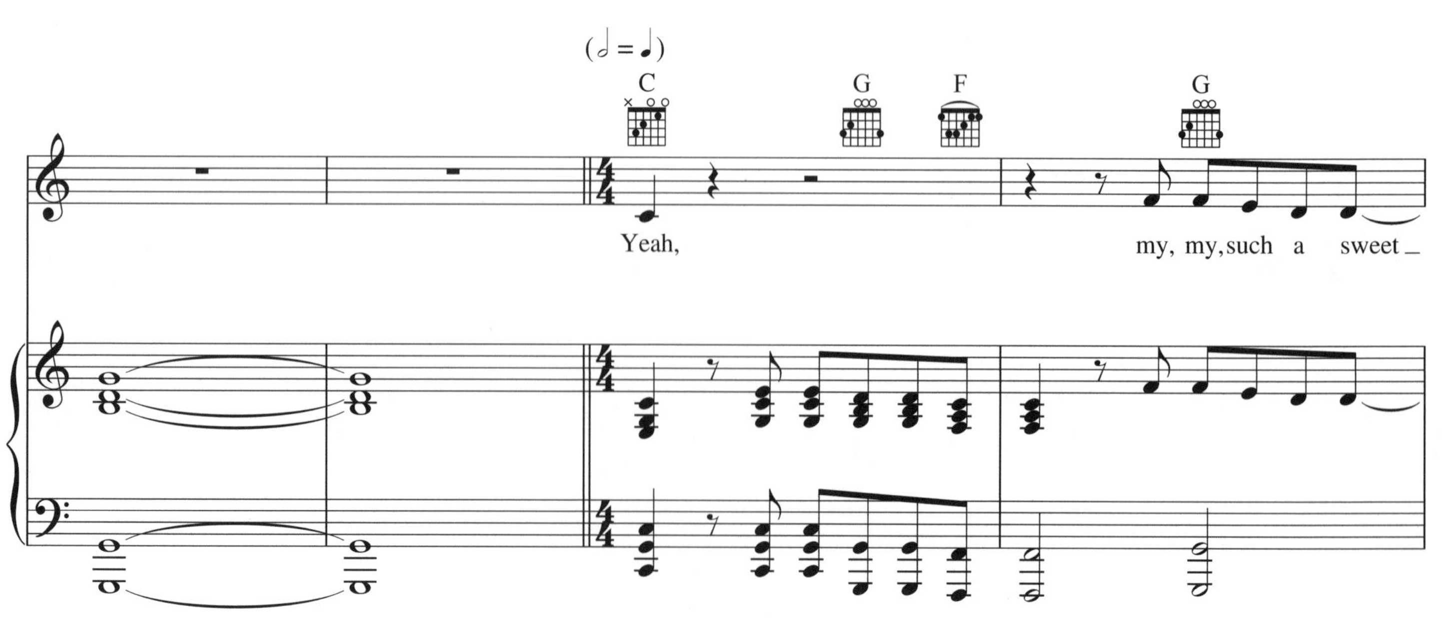

C
G
F
G
thing.
I wan-na do ev-er-y-
C
G
F
G
thing.
What a beau-ti-ful feel-
C
G
F
G
C
G
F
ing:
crim-son and clo-ver,
G
o-ver and o-ver.

C
G
F
G
C
G
Crim - son and clo - ver,
F
G
C
G
F
G
o - ver and o - ver. Crim - son and clo - ver, o - ver and o - ver.
C
G
F
G
C
G
F
G
C

Da Doo Ron Ron
(When He Walked Me Home)

Words and Music by
Ellie Greenwich, Jeff Barry
and Phil Spector

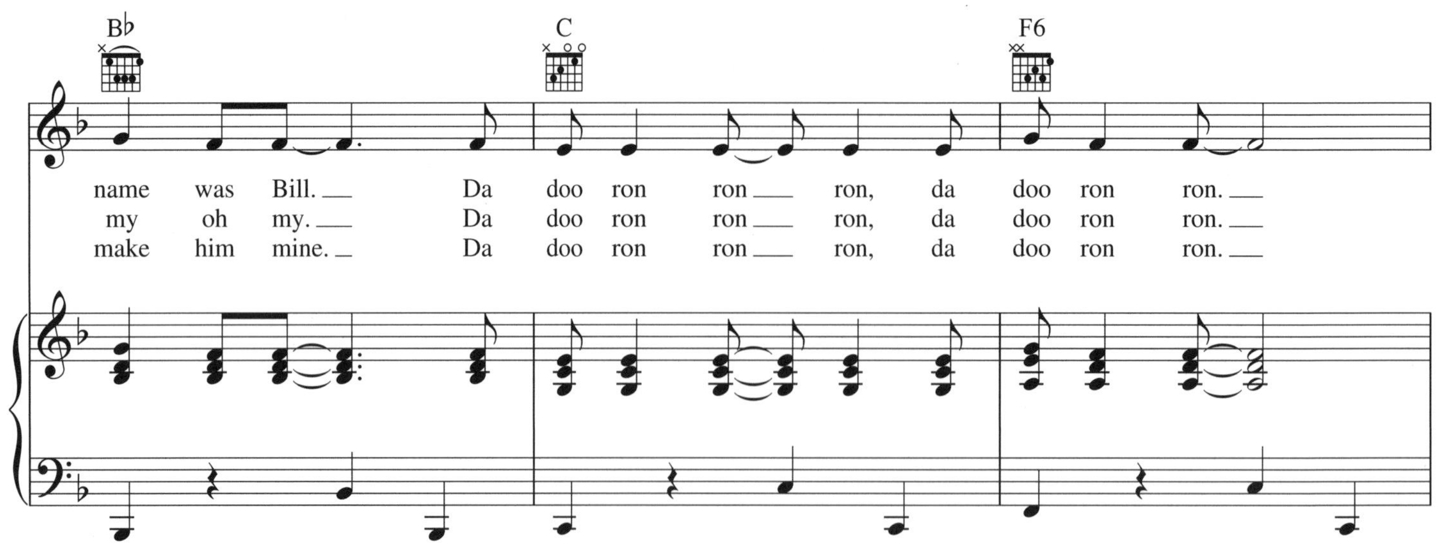
B♭
C
F6
name was Bill. Da doo ron ron ron, da doo ron ron.
my oh my. Da doo ron ron ron, da doo ron ron.
make him mine. Da doo ron ron ron, da doo ron ron.

F
B♭
F
Yes, my heart stood still. Yes, his
Yes, he caught my eye. Yes, but
Yes, he looked so fine. Yes, I'm gon - na

C7
F
B♭
name was Bill.
my oh my.
make him mine.
And when he walked me home, da

C
F6
1, 2
doo ron ron ron, da doo ron ron.

3
F
He
He
Yeah, yeah. Yeah,

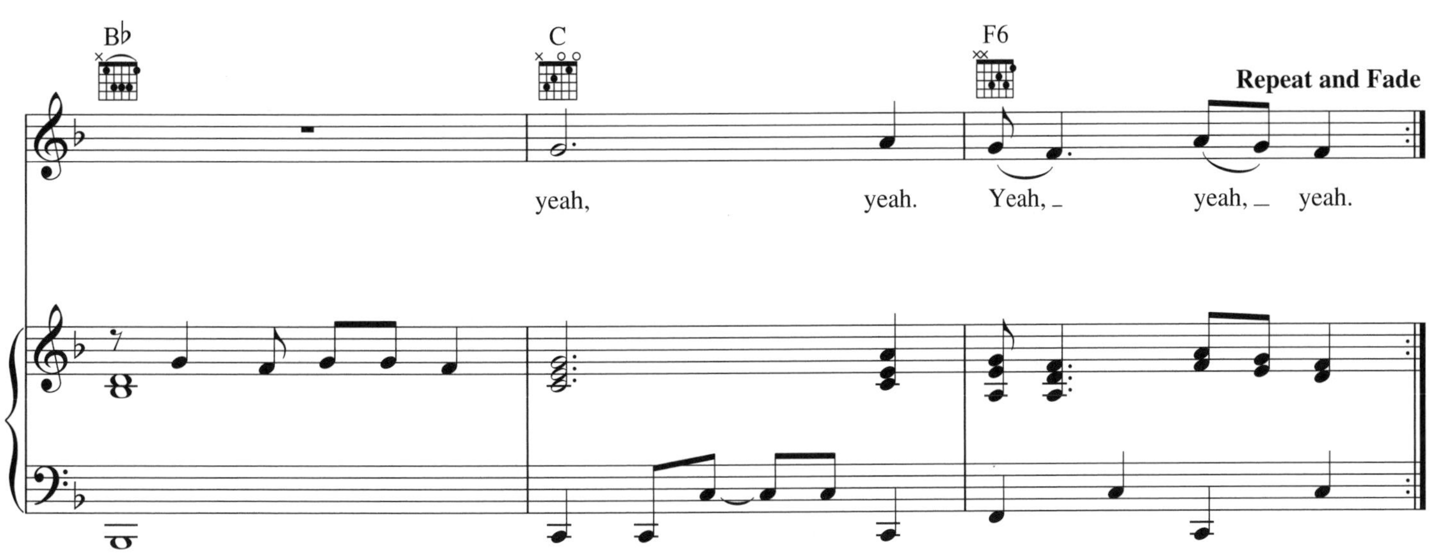
B♭
C
F6
Repeat and Fade
yeah, yeah. Yeah, yeah, yeah.

Daydream Believer

Words and Music by
John Stewart

2
F
Dm
Gm7
C7
F
shav - ing raz - or's cold and it stings.
Bb
C7
Am
Cheer up, sleep - y Jean.
Bb
C7
Dm
Bb
F
Oh, what can it mean to a day - dream be -
Bb
F
Dm
G7
liev - er and a home - com - ing queen.

C7 F Gm 3fr
You once thought of me as a
good times start and end with - out
Am B♭ 1 F
white knight on a steed. Now you know how
dol - lar one to spend. But
Dm G7 C7
hap - py I can be. Oh, and our
2 F Dm Gm7 C7 F
D.S. and Fade
how much, ba - by, do we real - ly need?

Do You Love Me

Words and Music by
Berry Gordy

F
B♭
C
B♭
love me? Do you love me? Now that
B♭m
C7
I can dance.
(Dance.)
N.C.
C7
F
Watch me now! Hey! Work! Work! Ah,
B♭
C
F
B♭
C
work it out, ba - by. Work! Work! Well, you're driv - in' me cra - zy.
3

F
B♭
C
F
N.C.
Work! Work! With just a lit - tle bit of soul now. Work!
C7
F
B♭
C
I can mash po - ta - to. I can mash po - ta - to. I can
F
B♭
C
F
do the twist. I can do the twist. Now tell me, ba - by.
B♭
C
F
B♭
C
Tell me, ba - by. Do you like it like this? Do you like it like this?

C7
Tell me! Tell me! Tell me!
F
Bb
C
Do you love me? Do you love me?
Now do you love me?
F
Bb
C
F
Do you love me?
Now do you love me?
Bb
C
To Coda
Bb
Bbm
Do you love me? Now that I can

C7
dance.
(Dance.)
N.C.
C7
F
B♭
C
Watch me now! Hey! Work! Work!
F
B♭
C
F
Work! Work!
Work! Work!
B♭
C
F
N.C.
1
C7
Work!

2
D.S. al Coda
C7
N.C.
I can
CODA
C7
Now,
now,
now.
N.C.
C7
F
Work! Work!
B♭
C
F
Work! Work!
B♭
C
Repeat and Fade
F
B♭
C
F
C7
N.C.
C7
Work! Work!
Work!

Do You Want to Dance?

Words and Music by
Bobby Freeman

Dmaj9
4fr
Gmaj7
Dmaj9
4fr
Gmaj7
3
We could dance un - der the moon - light; hug and kiss all through the night. Oh, _
3
F♯m7
Bm7
Em7
Em7/A
Dmaj9
4fr
(Ba - by.) _ (Dance.) _
ba - by, _ tell me, do you want to dance _ with me, ba - by?
Gmaj7
F♯m7
Em7
Em7/A
Dmaj9
4fr
G
Gmaj9
(Do you, do you?)
Do you, do you, do you, do you want _ to dance? _
Dmaj9
4fr
G
Gmaj9
F♯m7
Bm7
(Do you, do you, do you want _ to dance?) _ (Do you, do you?)
Do you, do you, do you want _ to dance? _ Do you do you, do you, do _

Em7 Em7/A Dmaj9 Gmaj9 F♯m7 Em7 Em7/A A7
you want to dance with me, ba - by? Ah, that's right!
cresc. poco a poco
Em7/A
Ah, ah, ah. Do you
f
F D♭9 C7 F Dm7 Gm7 Gm7♭5/C
dance? Well, do you want to dance and to make ro - mance?
F Dm7 Gm7 C7♭9 Gm7♭5/C F Dm7 Gm7 C7♭9
Kiss and squeeze? Mm yes! Do you want to

F
E♭9
F6
F
Dm7
Gm7
C7
dance?
Do you, do you, do you, do you
wan - na dance?
F
Dm7
Gm7
C7
F
Dm7
Do you, do you, do you, do you
wan - na dance?
Do you, do you, do you, do you
Gm7
C7♭9
F6
E♭9
F6
want to dance?
C7
C9
C7♭9
F6
mp cresc.
f

Down in the Boondocks

Words and Music by
Joe South

G
born in.
I love her,
she loves me,
but I don't fit in her so-
C
ci-e-ty,
Lord, have mer-cy on the
D
C
Bm
Am
G
boy from down in the boon-docks.
To Coda

C
Ev - 'ry night I watch the lights from the house up on the
One fine day I'll find a way to move from this old
G
hill. I love a girl who lives up there, and I
shack. I'll hold my head up like a king, and
Em
B7
guess I al - ways will. But
nev - er, nev - er will look back, un -
Em
Am7
I don't dare knock on her door 'cause her
til that morn - ing I'll work and slave And
D7

Am7
D7
Am7
dad - dy is my boss man. So I have to try to
I'll ___ save ev - 'ry dime. But to - night she'll have to
D7
Am7
be con - tent, just to see her when - ev - er I
steal a - way, to ___ see ___ me one ___ more
1
D7
2
D7
D.S. al Coda
can.
time.
CODA
D
Lord, have mer - cy on the
C
Bm
Am
G
Repeat and Fade
Optional Ending
boy from down in the boon - docks. ___

Ferry 'Cross the Mersey

Words and Music by
Gerard Marsden

C
Gm7
G7
C
Em
So fer - ry 'cross the Mer - sey 'cause this
So fer - ry 'cross the Mer - sey and
So fer - ry 'cross the Mer - sey 'cause this
Dm
G7
To Coda
1
C
Gm7
land's the place I love and here I'll stay.
al - ways take me there, the place I
land's the place I love and here I'll
C
Gm7
2
C
love.
Dm
G7
C
Dm
G7
Peo - ple a - round ev - 'ry cor - ner they seem to smile and

C
Dm
G7
G7/F
Em
say
we don't care what your
name is, boy,
D7
G7
D.S. al Coda
we'll nev - er send you a - way.
CODA
C
Gm7
stay,
C
Gm7
C
Gm7
C
Gm7
and here I'll
stay,
here I'll
C
Gm7
C
Gm7
C
stay.

Georgia on My Mind

Words by Stuart Gorrell

Music by Hoagy Carmichael

A7 D7 D7♯5 D7 G9 C7
9fr
blos - soms fall and all the world's a song,
F A7♯5 A7/D Dm G7 Edim7 C13 F
2fr
I'll go back to Geor - gia 'cause that's where I be - long.
F A7 Dm
Geor - gia, Geor - gia, the whole day
Gm B♭m F E7 Gm G9 C7 F F♯dim
3fr 3fr 9fr 9fr
through. Just an old sweet song keeps Geor - gia on my mind.

Gm7
C7♯5
8fr
F
A7
(Geor - gia on my mind.)
Geor - gia,
Geor - gia,
Dm
Gm
3fr
B♭m
F
E7
a song of you
comes as sweet and clear as
Gm
3fr
G9
9fr
C13
2fr
F
E♭9
F
A7
Dm
Gm6
3fr
moon - light through the pines.
Oth - er arms reach
Dm
B♭7
Dm
Gm6
3fr
Dm7
G7
out to me;
Oth - er eyes smile ten - der - ly;

Dm
Gm6
3fr
Dm7
E7
Am
F♯dim
9fr
Fm6
Still in peace - ful dreams I see the road leads back to
Dm
C7
F
A7
Dm
you. Geor- gia, Geor - gia, no peace I
Gm
3fr
B♭m
F
E7
Gm
3fr
G9
9fr
C13
2fr
find. Just an old sweet song keeps Geor - gia on my
1
F
Dm
Gm7
C13
2fr
C7♯5
8fr
2
F
B♭6/9
C7♯5
8fr
F6
mind. mind.
rit.

Goldfinger

from GOLDFINGER

Lyrics by
Leslie Bricusse and Anthony Newley

Music by John Barry

Moderately

F Db F Db

F Db

Gold - fin - ger!

Fmaj7 F Bb E

He's the man, the man with the Mi - das touch,

C C7 F Db

a spi - der's touch. Such a cold fin - ger

Fmaj7
F
B♭
beck - ons you to en - ter his web of
E
Am
F/A
Am6
F/A
sin. But don't go in. Gold - en
Em
B7
Em
words he will pour in your ear, but his lies can't dis - guise what you
B7♯9
E
Cm
fear. For a gold - en girl knows when he's kissed her.

Gm6
3fr
D♭dim7
F
D♭
It's the kiss of death from Mis - ter Gold - fin - ger.
Fmaj7
B♭
3
Pret - ty girl, be - ware of this heart of
E
gold. This heart is
1
Am
F/A
cold.
Am6
F/A
Gold - en
2
Am
F/A
cold.
Am6
F/A
He loves on - ly

Am
F/A
Am6
F/A
Am
F/A
gold, on - ly gold.
Am6
F/A
Am
F/A
Am6
F/A
He loves gold. He loves on - ly
3
Am
F/A
Am6
F/A
Am
F/A
gold, on - ly gold.
Am6
F/A
Am
F/A
Am6
F/A
Am6(add9)
4fr
He loves gold. He loves gold.

Good Morning Starshine

from the Broadway Musical Producion HAIR

Words by
James Rado and Gerome Ragni

Music by Galt MacDermot

C
D
C
D
C
D
Star - shine, You lead us a - long,
C
B7
Em
G7
C
B♭7
My love and me as we sing our
A7
D11
5fr
G
ear - ly morn - ing sing - ing song. Glid - dy glup gloo - py Nib -
f
Am7
D7
Am7
D7
- by nab - by noo - py La la la lo lo.

Am
D7
Am
D7
G
Sab - ba sib - by sab - ba Noo - by ab - ba nab - ba Le le lo lo.
G7
C
F#m/B
Em7
B7
Too - by oo - by wal - la Noo - by ab - ba nab - ba,
Em
Am
1
G
N.C.
2
G
Ear - ly morn - ing sing - ing song. Good Morn - ing
mp
Am7
D7
Sing - ing a song, Hum - ming a song, Sing - ing a song,
mf

Am7 D7 Am D7 Am D7
Lov - ing a song, Laugh - ing a song,
G G7 C F♯m/B
Sing the song Sing the song,
Em7 B7 Em Am D7
Song the sing. Song, song, song, sing, sing, sing, sing
G C G
Repeat and Fade
song.

Happy Together

Words and Music by
Garry Bonner and Alan Gordon

2
B
geth - er.
E
Bm7
E
I can see me lov - in' no - bod - y but you for all my life.
G
E
Bm7
When you're with me, ba - by, the skies - 'll be
E
G
Em
blue for all my life.
Me and you, and you and
3

D
me, no mat - ter how they toss the dice, it had to be. The on - ly one for
C
To Coda
B
me is you, and you for me, so hap - py to - geth - er.
E
Bm7
Ba ba ba ba ba ba
E
G
E
ba ba ba ba ba. Ba ba ba ba

Bm7
E
Bm7
D.S. al Coda
(no repeats)
ba ba ba ba ba ba ba.
3
CODA
B
Em
B
geth - er, so hap - py to - geth - er.
Em
B
Em
B
Repeat ad lib.
And how is the weath - er? So hap - py to - geth - er.
Em
B
E
So hap - py to - geth - er.

Harper Valley P.T.A.

Words and Music by
Tom T. Hall

D7
High. Well, her daugh-ter came home _ one af - ter -
wild. And we don't be - lieve you ought to be a -
room. And as she walked up to the black-board, I
noon and did - n't e - ven stop to play. She said,
bring - ing up your lit - tle girl this way." It was
still re - call the words she had to say. She said, "I'd
G7
A7
"Mom, I got _ a note _ here from the Har - per Val - ley P. T. A." _
signed by the sec - re - tar - y, Har - per Val - ley P. T. A. _
like to ad - dress this meet - ing of the Har - per Val - ley P. T.
D7
1, 2
3
B♭7
The
Well, it
A. Well, there's

E♭7
Bob - by Tay - lor sit - tin' there, and sev - en times he's asked me for a date.
Har - per could - n't be here 'cause he stayed too long at Kel - ly's Bar a - gain.
A♭7
4fr
Mis - sus Tay - lor sure seems to use a lot of
And if you smell Shir - ley Thomp - son's breath, you'll
ice when - ev - er he's a - way. And Mis - ter
find she's had a lit - tle nip of gin. Then you
E♭7
Bak - er, can you tell us why your sec - re - tar - y had to leave this town?
have the nerve to tell me you think that, as a moth - er, I'm not fit?
would - n't put you on, be - cause it real - ly did, it hap - pened just this way

Ab7
4fr
Bb7
And shouldn't widow Jones be told to keep her window shades all pulled completely
Well, this is just a little Peyton Place, and you're all Harper Valley hypo-
the day my mama socked it to the Harper Valley P. T.
Eb7
To Coda
1
2
D.S. al Coda
down?
crites."
A.
Well, Mister
No, I
CODA
Ab7
4fr
The day my mama socked it to the
Bb7
Eb7
Harper Valley P. T. A.

Heatwave
(Love Is Like a Heatwave)

Words and Music by
Edward Holland, Lamont Dozier
and Brian Holland

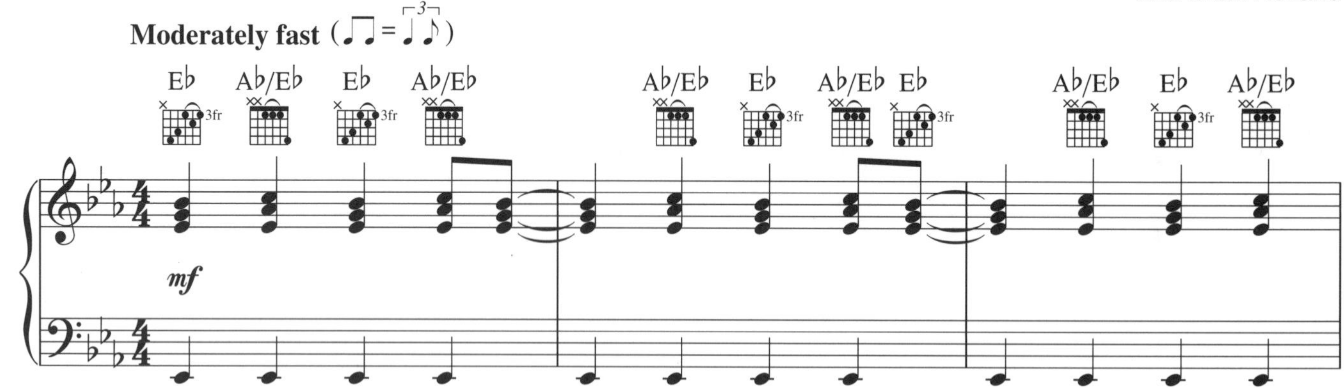

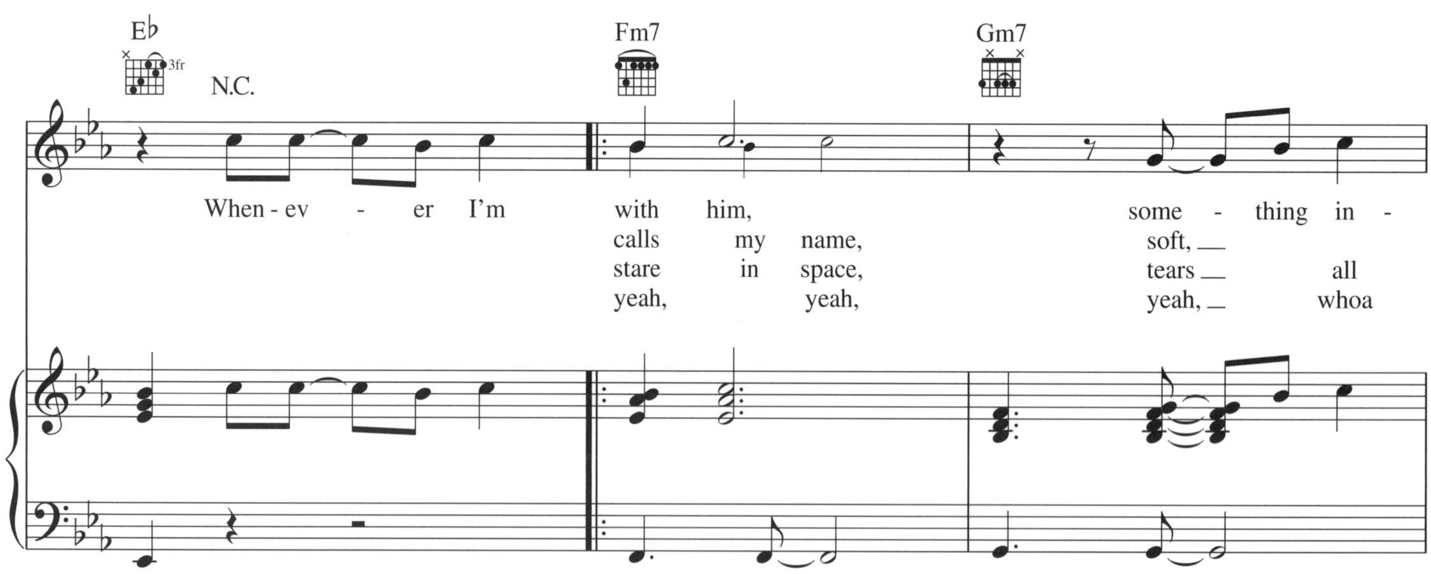

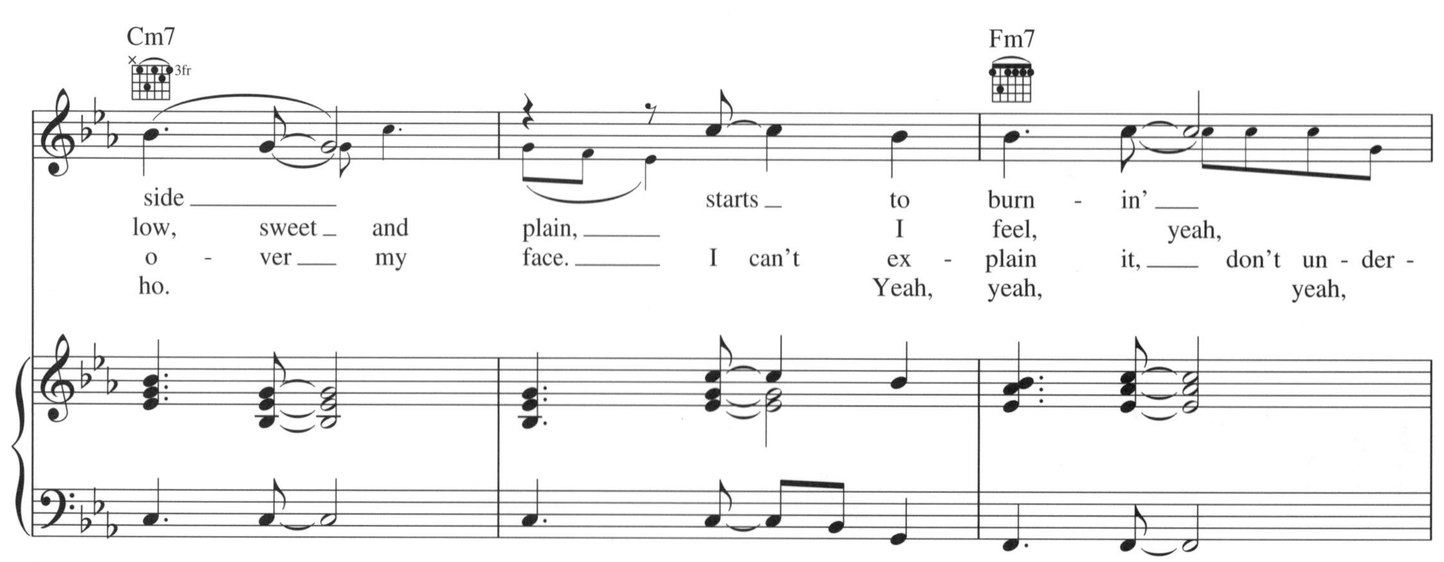

Gm7
Cm7
and I'm filled with de - sire.
yeah, well, I feel that burn - in' flame. Has
stand it. I ain't nev - er felt like this be - fore. Now
yeah, ho, yeah.

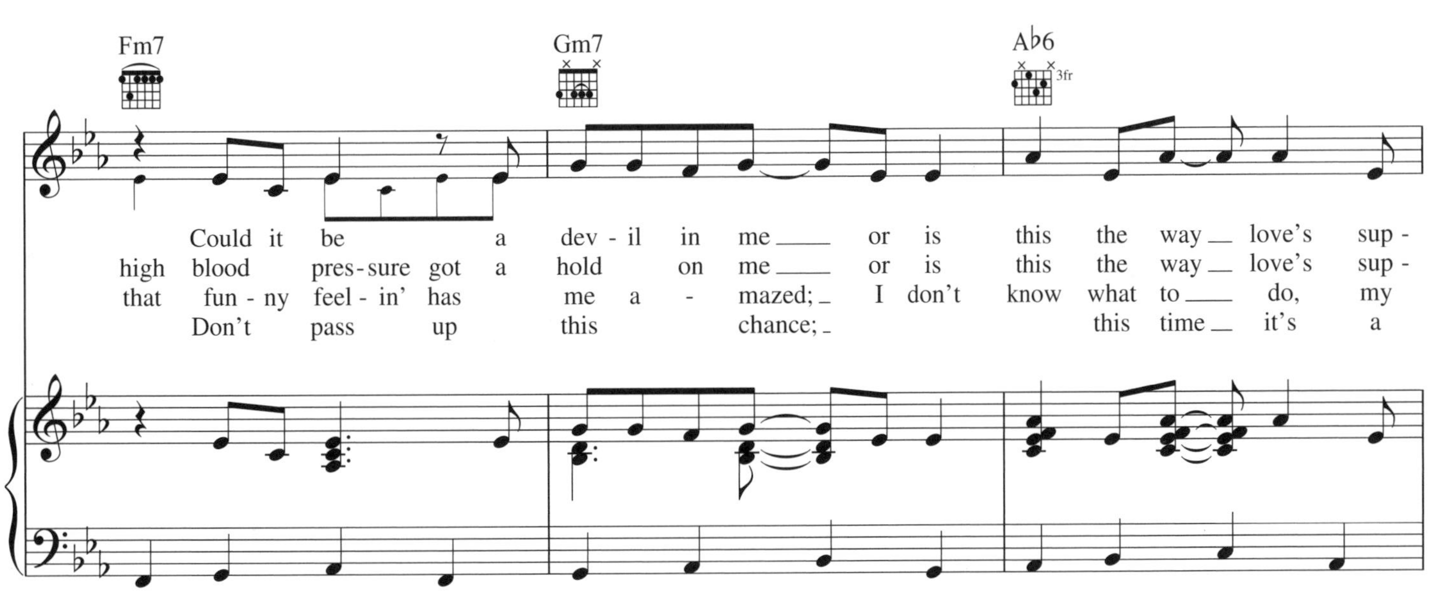
Fm7
Gm7
A♭6
Could it be a dev - il in me or is this the way love's sup -
high blood pres - sure got a hold on me or is this the way love's sup -
that fun - ny feel - in' has me a - mazed; I don't know what to do, my
Don't pass up this chance; this time it's a

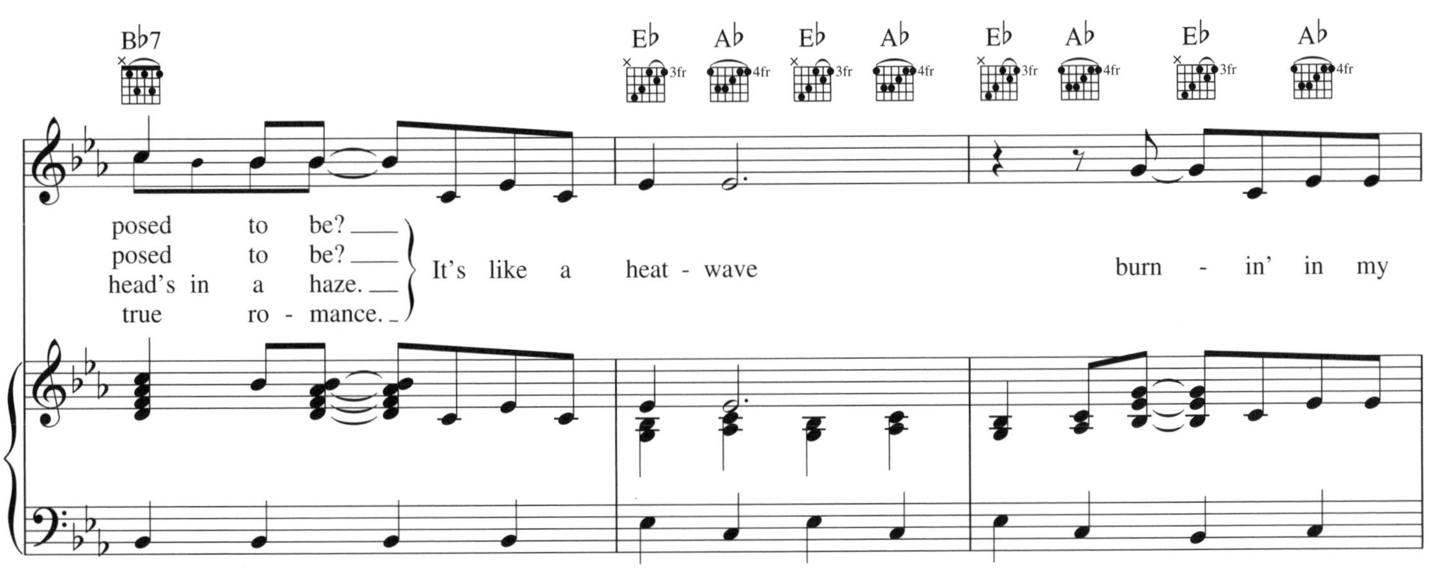
B♭7
E♭ A♭ E♭ A♭ E♭ A♭ E♭ A♭
posed to be?
posed to be?
head's in a haze.
true ro - mance.
It's like a heat - wave burn - in' in my

E♭
A♭
3fr
4fr
heart.
I can't keep from cry - in',
it's tear - in' me a - part.
1-3
N.C.
When - ev - er he
Some - times I
Yeah, yeah, yeah,
4
Fm7
Gm7
A♭6
B♭7

Hey Jude

Words and Music by
John Lennon and Paul McCartney

C7
F
to make it bet - ter.
Hey
F
C
C7
C7sus
C7
Jude, don't be a - fraid. You were made to go out and
Jude, don't let me down. You have found her, now go and
F
B♭
get her. The min - ute you let her un - der your
get her. Re - mem - ber to let her in - to your
F
C7
F
skin, then you be - gin to make it bet - ter.
heart; then you can start to make it bet - ter.

F7
Bb
Bb/A
And an - y - time you feel the pain, hey Jude, re - frain;
So let it out and let it in. Hey Jude, be - gin;
Gm7
Gm7/F
C7/E
C7
F
don't car - ry the world up - on your shoul - ders.
you're wait - ing for some - one to per - form with.
F7
Bb
Bb/A
For well you know that it's a fool who plays it cool
And don't you know that it's just you? Hey Jude, you'll do.
Gm7
Gm7/F
C7/E
C7
by mak - ing his world a lit - tle cold -
The move - ment you need is on your shoul -

F
F7
C7
er.
der.
Da da da da da da da da da.
1
2
D.S. al Coda
Hey
Hey Jude,
CODA
C7
to make it bet -
F
ter, bet - ter, bet - ter, bet - ter, bet - ter, bet - ter, oh.
Da da da
E♭
3fr
B♭
F
Repeat and Fade
Optional Ending
da da da da,
da da da da,
hey Jude.

Hey There Lonely Girl

(Hey There Lonely Boy)

Words and Music by
Leon Carr and Earl Shuman

G
N.C.
Bm
C
Ev - er since he broke your heart, you seem so lost, each time you
lips can kiss your lips and make your
D
N.C.
Bm
pass my way. Oh, how I long to take your hand, and say don't
heart stand still; But once you're in my arms you'll see no one can
C
D
cry, I'll kiss your tears a - way. Hey there
kiss your lips the way I will.
Cmaj7
Bm7
2fr
Am7
lone - ly girl, lone - ly girl, let me make your bro - ken heart like

Gmaj7
G
Cmaj7
Bm7
2 fr
new.
Hey there lone - ly girl,
lone - ly girl,
Am7
1
G
C
G
N.C.
don't you know this lone - ly boy loves you?
You think that on - ly his two
2 G
Cmaj7
Bm7
2 fr
you?
Hey there lone - ly girl,
lone - ly girl,
Am7
G
C
G
don't you know this lone - ly boy loves you?

Hot Fun in the Summertime

Words and Music by
Sylvester Stewart

Dm7
G7
Them sum - mer days,
G9
9fr
Dm7
C/E
F
Am7
those sum - mer days.
G7
Dm7/G
C/G
F/G
C
That's when I had
First of the fall
Gm9
3fr
Dm7♭5
most of my fun back.
and there she goes back.

Ab(add9) Gm7 Fm7 Eb(add9) Eb
Hi, hi, hi, hi there. Them
Bye, bye, bye, bye there. Them
Dm7 G9
sum - mer days, those sum - mer days.
sum - mer days, those sum - mer days.
Dm7 C/E F Am7 G
I cloud nine when I
Ba ba ba ba ba when I
Dm7 C/E F Am7 G
want to! Out of school,
want to! Out of school,

Dm7 C/E F Am7 G
coun - ty fair in the coun -
coun - ty fair in the coun -
Dm7 C/E F Am7 G
- try sun, and ev - 'ry - thing is
- try sun, and ev - 'ry - thing is
Dm7 C/E F Am7 G Em7
cool.
cool.
1
Dm7 C/E F Am7 G7
Hot fun in the sum - mer - time!

Dm7
C/E
F
Am7
G7
Hot fun in the sum - mer - time!
Dm7
C/E
F
Am7
G7
Hot fun in the sum - mer - time!
Dm7
C/E
F
Am7
G7
Hot fun in the sum - mer - time!
2
Dm7
C/E
F
Am7
G7
Repeat and Fade
Optional Ending
C
Hot fun in the sum - mer - time!

How Can I Be Sure

Words and Music by
Felix Cavaliere and Edward Brigati, Jr.

F
Em
D
where I stand with you?
Dm
Dm(maj7)
Dm7
When - ev - er I, when - ev - er
I, when - ev - er
Dm6
Em7♭5
A7
Em7♭5
I, I'm a - way from you,
I, I'm a - way from you,
A7
Dm
Dm(maj7)
Dm7
I want to die 'cause you
my al - i - bi is tell - in'

Dm6
Em7♭5
A7
Em7♭5
know I wan - na stay with you.
peo - ple I don't care for you.
A7
F♯m7
Bm7
Em7
How do I know? May - be you're
May - be I'm just hang - ing a -
A7
F♯m7
Bm7
Em7
try - ing to use me, fly - ing too
round with my head up, up - side
A7
Fmaj7
1
Dm
Gm7
Gm6
3fr
high can con - fuse me. Touch me, but don't take me
down. It's a pit -

D
down.
When - ev - er
2
Dm
Gm7
C7
Fmaj7
y.
I
can't
seem
to
find
some - one
who's
Dm7
Gm7
C7
D
as
pret - ty
and
love - ly
as
you.
C
How
can
I
be

D
C
sure?
I really, really, really want to
D
C
know,
I really, really, really want to
D
F#m7
Bm7
know.
How's the weath - er?
Em7
A7
F#m7
Bm7
Weath - er or not we're to - geth - er. To -

Em7
A7
Fmaj7
Dm7
geth - er we'll see it much bet - ter. I
Gm7
C7
Fmaj7
Dm7
Gm7
love you, I love you for - ev - er, you know where
C7
D
D.S. al Coda
I can be found.
CODA
F
Em
D
I'll be sure with you.
rit.

I Can't Help Myself
(Sugar Pie, Honey Bunch)

Words and Music by
Brian Holland, Lamont Dozier
and Edward Holland

Em
F
G
I love you and no - bod - y else.
I'm a fool in love you see.
Wan - na
C
In and out my life you come and you go,
tell you I don't love you, tell you that we're through, and I've tried.
G
Dm
leav - ing just your pic - ture be - hind
But ev - 'ry time I see your face
Em
F
and I kissed it a thou - sand times.
I get all choked up in - side.

To Coda
G
C
When you snap your fin - ger or wink your eye, I come a -
When
G
Dm
run - ning to you. I'm tied to your a - pron strings
Em
F
and there's noth - ing that I can do.
G
C

G
Dm
Can't help my - self,
Em
F
G
D.S. al Coda
no, I can't help my - self.
CODA
C
I call your name, girl, it starts the flame burn -
- ing in my heart, tear - ing it all a - part. No mat -

- ter how I try, my love I can - not hide. 'Cause
C
sug - ar pie, hon - ey bunch, you know that I'm
Sug - ar pie, hon - ey bunch, do an - y - thing you
G
Dm
weak for you. Can't help my - self,
ask me to. Can't help my - self,
F
G
Repeat and Fade
Optional Ending
I love you and no-bod - y else.
I want you and no-bod - y else.

I Got You Babe

Words and Music by
Sonny Bono

F
B♭
E♭
3fr
C
Gm7
C7
you got me, and ba - by, I got you,

F
B♭
F
B♭
babe, I got you, babe. I got

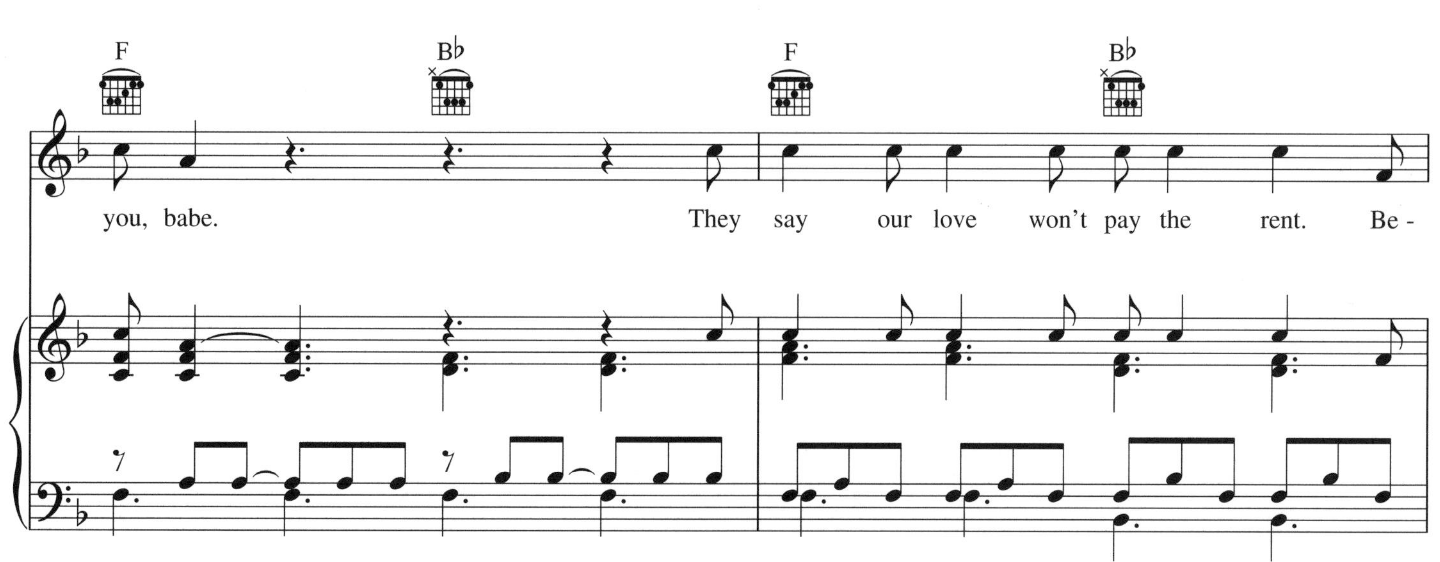
F
B♭
F
B♭
you, babe. They say our love won't pay the rent. Be -

F
E♭
3fr
C
Gm7
C7
fore it's earned, our mon-ey's all been spent.
I
F
B♭
F
E♭
3fr
guess that's so, we don't have a pot. But at least I'm sure of all the things we
C
Gm7
C7
F
B♭
got, babe,
I got
F
B♭
F
you, babe.
I got you, babe.
I got

Gm
3fr
Gm7
C7
flow - ers in the spring, I got
Gm
3fr
Gm7
C7
F
you to wear my ring. And when I'm
Gm7
sad, you're a clown; and if I get
F
C7
C♯7
scared, you're al - ways a - round. So

F♯
B
F♯
E
let them say your hair's too long, 'cause I don't care. With you I can't do
C♯
G♯m7
4fr
C♯7
F♯
B
wrong.
Then put your lit - tle hand in mine.
F♯
E
C♯
G♯m7
4fr
C♯7
There ain't no hill or moun - tain we can't climb,
F♯
B
F♯
B
Repeat and Fade
babe,
I got you, babe.
I got

I Say a Little Prayer

Lyric by Hal David

Music by Burt Bacharach

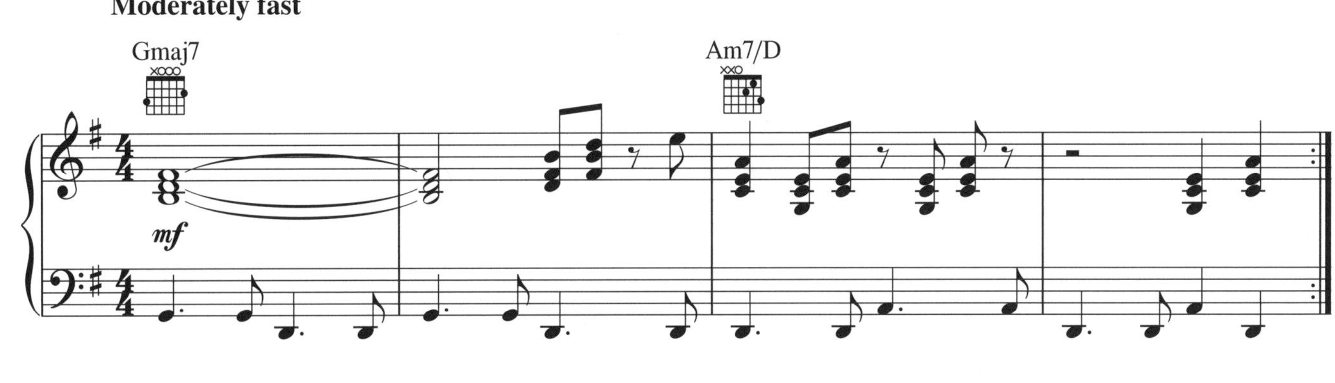

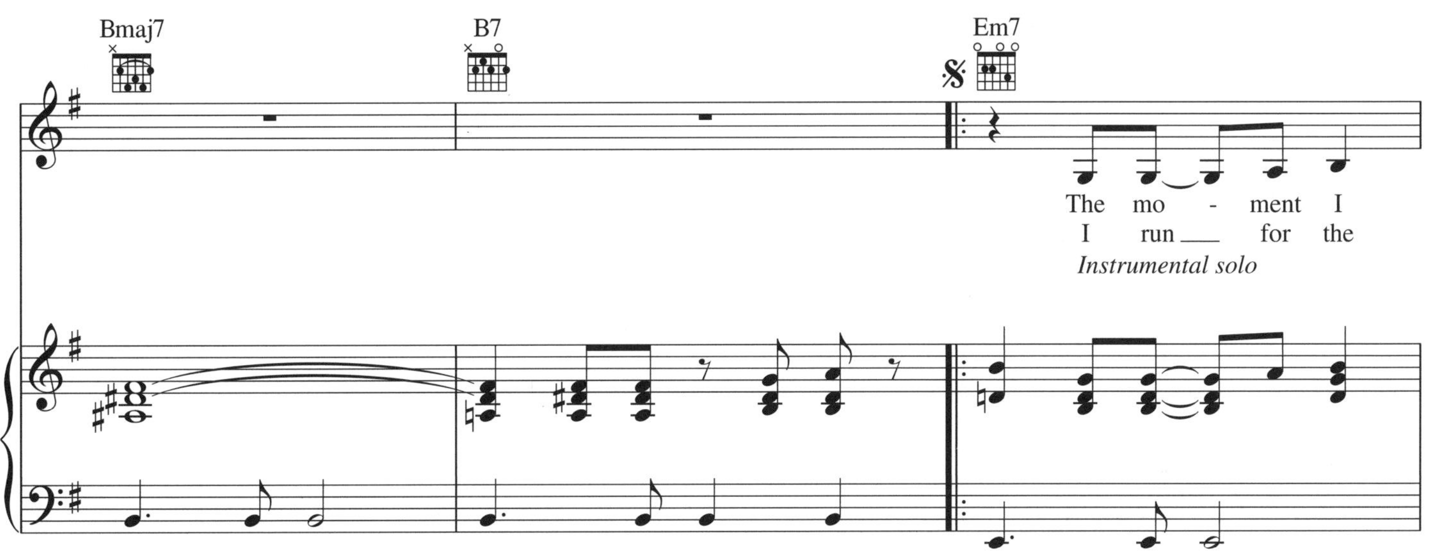

F♯m7
B
say a lit - tle prayer for you.
say a lit - tle prayer for you.
say a lit - tle prayer for you.)
Solo continues
Em7
Am7
While comb - ing my hair now, and won - d'ring what
At work, I just take time, and all through my
D
Gmaj7
F♯m7
dress to wear now,
cof - fee break time,
End solo
I say a lit - tle prayer for you.
B
C
D/C
For - ev - er, for - ev - er, you'll

Bm7 G/B F/G G C D/C
stay in my heart and I will love you. For - ev - er and ev - er, we
Bm7 G/B F/G G F/G G C D/C
nev - er will part. Oh, how I'll love you. To - geth - er, to - geth - er, that's
Bm7 G/B F/G G C D/C
how it must be. To live with - out you would on - ly mean heart - break for
B
To Coda
1
2
D.S. al Coda
me.

CODA
Em7
Am7
My dar - ling, be - lieve me,
C/D
for me there is no one but
Gmaj7
Am7/D
Gmaj7
you.
Please love me, too.
Am7/D
Gmaj7
Am7/D
I'm in love with you, an - swer my

Gmaj7
Am7/D
Gmaj7
prayer.
Say you love me, too.
Am7/D
Gmaj7
Why don't you an - swer my prayer?
prayer.
Am7/D
Repeat and Fade
You know, ev - 'ry day I say a lit - tle

Jean

Words and Music by
Rod McKuen

Fm7
B♭11
E♭
Fm7
B♭7
come out to the mead - ow, Jean.
E♭
Gm
A♭
B♭7
Jean, Jean, you're young and a - live.
E♭
Cm
Fm7
B♭7
Come out of your half - dreamed dream, and
E♭
E♭7
A♭
E♭
run, if you will, to the top of the hill.

Fm7
B♭11
E♭
E♭7
O - pen your arms, bon - nie Jean. Till the
A♭6
Adim
E♭maj7
E♭7
sheep in the val - ley come home my way, till the
A♭6
Adim
E♭maj7
E♭7
stars fall a - round me and find me a - lone, when the
A♭
A♭6
Gm7
Cm7
C♭7
B♭7
sun comes a - sing - in', I'll still be wait - in'.

E♭
Gm
A♭
B♭7
Jean, Jean, the ros - es are red;
E♭
Cm
Fm7
B♭7
all the leaves have gone green. And the
E♭6
E♭7
A♭
E♭
Fm7
hills are a - blaze with the moon's yel - low haze. Come in - to my
B♭11
1
E♭
E♭7
2
E♭
arms, bon - nie Jean. Till the Jean.
rall.

Jimmy Mack

Words and Music by
Brian Holland, Lamont Dozier
and Edward Holland

D
G/D
D
G/D
D
G/D
coming a - round he's try - ing to wear my re - sist - ance down. Hey,
G6
Em
D
Jim - my, Jim - my oh, Jim - my Mack, when are you
G
Em
com - ing back? Jim - my, Jim - my, oh,
D
1
G
A
Jim - my Mack, you bet - ter hur - ry back.

Additional Lyrics

2. He calls me on the phone about three times a day
Now my heart's just listening to what he has to say.
But this loneliness I have within
Keeps reaching out to be his friend.
Hey, Jimmy, Jimmy oh Jimmy Mack,
When are you coming back?
Jimmy, Jimmy oh Jimmy Mack, you better hurry back.

Knock on Wood

A
is bet - ter
than an - y love I know.
E
A
It's like thun - der,
light - ning;
E
A
E
the way you love me is fright - 'ning. I think I bet - ter knock knock knock knock knock on wood.
To Coda
G
A
B
D
1
B
A
G
I'm not su - per
f

Additional Lyrics

3. Ain't no secret that a woman can feel my love come up.
   You got me seeing, she really sees that, that I get enough.
   Just one touch from you, baby, you know it means so much.
   It's like thunder, lightning;
   The way you love me is frightening.
   I think I better knock knock knock knock knock on wood.

King of the Road

Words and Music by
Roger Miller

F
G
To Coda
1
C
N.C.
man of means by no means, king of the road.
2
C
G
C
F
G7
I know ev-er-y en-gi-neer on ev-er-y train, all of the chil-dren and
C
F
all of their names, and ev-er-y hand-out in ev-er-y town, and
G7
N.C.
D.S. al Coda
ev-'ry lock that ain't locked when no one's a-round. I sing:
CODA
C

Last Train to Clarksville

Words and Music by
Bobby Hart and Tommy Boyce

C7
slow.
Oh...
Oh, no, no, no!
Oh, no, no, no!
'Cause I'm
Take the
G7
leav - ing in the morn - ing and I must see you a -
last train to Clarks - ville, now I must hang up the
gain. We'll have one more night to - geth - er 'til the
phone. I can't hear you in this nois - y rail - road

C7
morn - ing brings my train. And I must go.
sta - tion all a - lone I'm feel - in' low.
Oh, no, no, no!
Oh, no, no, no!
D7
And I don't know if I'm ev - er com - ing
G
home.
2nd time D.S. and Fade
Take the

Lemon Tree

Words and Music by
Will Holt

Dm Dm/C Gm7 C7 F
les - son from the love - ly lem - on tree." "Don't
when she smiled the stars rose in the sky. We
left be - hind I knew what she had done. She'd
Bb Ab Bb Ab Bb Ab Gm
4fr.
put your faith in love, my boy," my fa - ther said to me. "I
passed that sum - mer lost in love be - neath the lem - on tree. The
left me for an - oth - er, it's a com - mon tale, but true. A
Gb Bb Cm7 F7 Bb7
chorus:
fear you'll find that love is like the love - ly, lem - on tree.
mu - sic of her laugh - ter hid my fa - ther's words from me.
sad - der man but wis - er now, I sing these words to you.
Lem - on
poco rit.

E♭
tree very - y pret - ty, and the lem - on flow - er is
mf a tempo
B♭7
sweet. But the fruit of the poor lem - on is im -
E♭
pos - si - ble to eat. Lem - on tree ver - y
B♭7
pret - ty, and the lem - on flow - er is sweet. But the

fruit of the poor lem - on is im - pos - si - ble to
1.2.
3.
E♭
C7
eat.
2. One
3. One
eat. Lem - on
B♭7
E♭
tree, lem - on tree. Lem - on
B♭7
E♭
tree, lem - on tree.
mp
p

Like a Rolling Stone

Words and Music by
Bob Dylan

G
a - kid - din' you.
used to it.
kicks for you.
F
G
You used to laugh a - bout
You say you nev - er com - pro - mise
You used to ride on a chrome horse with your dip - lo - mat
F
G
ev - 'ry - bod - y that was hang - in' out.
with the mys - ter - y tramp, but now you re - al - ize
who car - ried on his shoul - der a Sia - mese cat.
F Em Dm C F Em
But now you don't talk so loud. Now you don't
he's not sell - ing an - y al - i - bis as you stare in - to the vac - uum
Ain't it hard when you dis - cov - er that he real - ly was - n't

Dm
C
Dm
F
seem so proud a - bout hav-in' to be scroung-ing for your next
of his eyes and say, "Do you want to make a
where it's at af - ter he took from you ev - 'ry-thing he could
G
Chorus
C
F
meal.
deal?"
steal.
How does it feel?
How does it feel?
G
C
F
G
How does it feel to be with-out a home,
How does it feel to be on your own,
C
F
G
C
F
like a com-plete un - known,
with no di - rec - tion home,

1
G
C
F
G
like a roll-ing stone?
C
F
G
Oh, you've
2, 3
G
C
F
G
a com-plete un - known,
like a roll - ing stone?
C
F
G
C
F

Additional Lyrics

4. Princess on the steeple and all the pretty people
They're all drinkin', thinkin' that they got it made.
Exchanging all precious gifts,
But you better take your diamond ring,
You'd better pawn it, babe.
You used to be so amused
At Napoleon in rags and the language that he used.
Go to him now, he calls you, you can't refuse.
When you got nothin', you got nothin' to lose.
You're invisible now, you got no secrets to conceal.
Chorus

Let's Twist Again

Words by Kal Mann

Music by
Dave Appell and Kal Mann

C7
F
C
Ee - ah 'roun' 'n a 'roun' 'n a up 'n down we go a -
F
F♯
G7
gain. Oh, ba - by, make me know you love me so, an'
C
Am
then let's twist a - gain, like we did last sum - mer.
F
G
C
Yeah, let's twist a - gain, like we did last year.

Mack the Knife

from THE THREEPENNY OPERA

English Words by Marc Blitzstein
Original German Words by Bert Brecht

Music by Kurt Weill

C6
G9
C6
Dm
9fr
sight. When the shark bites with his teeth, dear,
Dm7
G9
C6
C
9fr
scar - let bil - lows start to spread. Fan - cy
Am
Am7
Dm7
gloves, though, wears Mac - heath, dear, so there's
G7
C6
G9
9fr
not a trace of red. On the

C6
Dm
Dm7
side - walk Sun - day morn - ing lies a
Mil - ler dis - ap - peared, dear, af - ter
G9
9fr
C6
bod - y ooz - ing life; some - one's
draw - ing out his cash; and Mac -
Am
Am7
Dm7
sneak - ing 'round the cor - ner. Is the
heath spends like a sail - or. Did our
G7
C6
G9
9fr
some - one Mack the Knife? From a
boy do some - thing rash? Su - key

C6
Dm
Dm7
tug - boat by the riv - er a ce -
Taw - dry, Jen - ny Div - er, Pol - ly
G9
9fr
C6
ment bag's drop - ping down; the ce -
Peach - um, Lu - cy Brown; oh, the
Am
Am7
Dm7
ment's just for the weight, dear. Bet you Mack - ie's
line forms on the right, dear, now that Mack - ie's
G7
1
C6
G9
9fr
2
C6
back in town. Lou - ie
back in town.
rall.

My Love

Words and Music by
Tony Hatch

F
My love is bright - er than the
Dm7
G7
Em
Am
bright - est star that shines ev - 'ry night a - bove and there is
Dm7
G7
To Coda
Dm7
G7
noth - ing in this world that can ev - er change my
C
G7
Dm7
love.

G7
C
F
Some - thing hap - pened to my heart the
Once I thought that love was meant for
G7
C
day that I met you,
an - y - one else but me.
some - thing that I
Once I thought you'd
F
G7
nev - er felt be - fore.
nev - er come my way.
C
F
G7
You are al - ways on my mind no mat - ter what I
Now it on - ly goes to show how wrong we all can

E7
A7
Dm7
G7
do, and ev - 'ry day it seems I want you
be, for now I have to tell you ev - 'ry
C
1
2
D.S. al Coda
more. My love is
day. My love is
CODA
Dm7
G7
C
change my love.
F
G7
C

Na Na Hey Hey Kiss Him Goodbye

Words and Music by
Gary De Carlo, Dale Frashuer
and Paul Leka

Bb
A7
Dm7
G7
He might be thrill - ing ba - by, but my love's so dog - gone will - ing so
F
Bb
Bbm
C6
F
kiss him, go on and kiss him good - bye. Na na
Ab
1
Eb
F
C7
2
Eb
F
C7
na na, hey hey hey, good - bye. Na na hey, hey good - bye. Na na
Repeat and Fade
F
Ab
Eb
F
C7
na na, na na na na, hey hey hey, good - bye. Na na

Ode to Billy Joe

Words and Music by
Bobbie Gentry

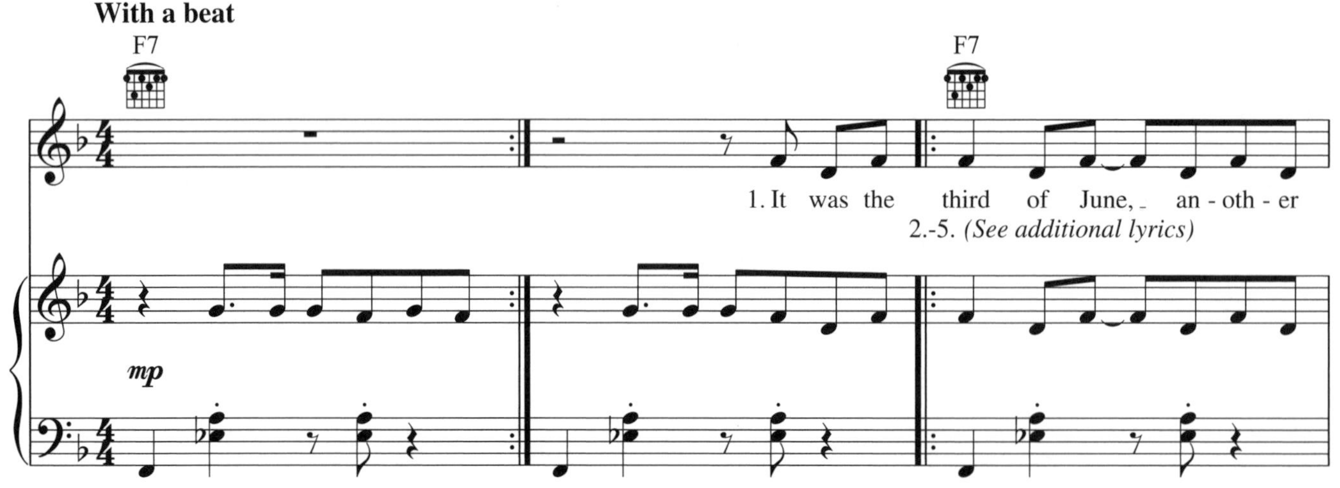

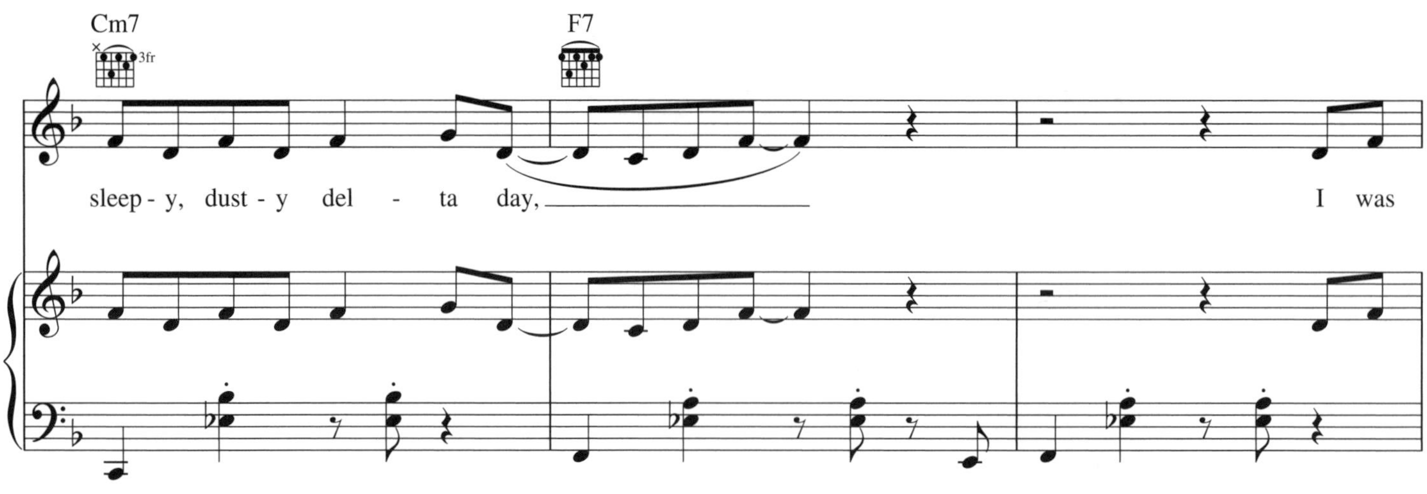

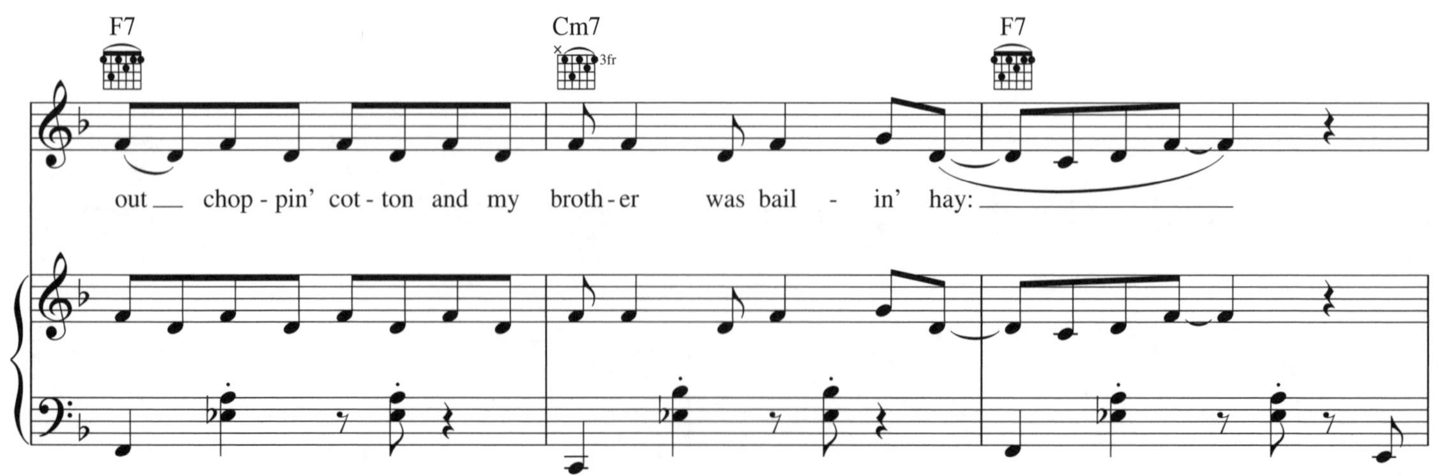

B♭7
And at din-ner time we stopped and walked back to the house to eat,
F7
Cm7
3fr
And Ma-ma hol-lered at the back door, "Y'all re-mem-ber to wipe your feet".
F7
B♭7
Then she said, "I got some news this morn-in' from Choc-taw Ridge,
To-day

Additional Lyrics

2. Papa said to Mama, as he passed around the black-eyed peas,
"Well, Billy Joe never had a lick o' sense, pass the biscuits, please.
There's five more acres in the lower forty I've got to plow,"
And Mama said it was a shame about Billy Joe anyhow.
Seems like nothin' ever comes to no good up on Choctaw Ridge,
And now Billy Joe McAllister's jumped off the Tallahatchee Bridge.

3. Brother said he recollected when he and Tom and Billy Joe
Put a frog down my back at the Carroll County picture show,
And wasn't talkin' to him after church last Sunday night,
I'll have another piece of apple pie, you know, it don't seem right.
I saw him at the sawmill yesterday on Choctaw Ridge,
And now you tell me Billy Joe's jumped off the Tallahatchee Bridge.

4. Mama said to me, "Child, what's happened to your appetite?
I been cookin' all mornin' and you haven't touched a single bite.
That nice young preacher Brother Taylor dropped by today,
Said he'd be pleased to have dinner on Sunday. Oh, by the way,
He said he saw a girl that looked a lot like you up on Choctaw Ridge
And she an' Billy Joe was throwin' somethin' off the Tallahatchee Bridge."

5. A year has come and gone since we heard the news 'bout Billy Joe,
Brother married Becky Thompson, they bought a store in Tupeolo.
There was a virus goin' 'round, Papa caught it and he died last spring,
And now Mama doesn't seem to want to do much of anything.
And me I spend a lot of time pickin' flowers up on Choctaw Ridge,
And drop them into the muddy water off the Tallahatchee Bridge.

Oh Happy Day

Words and Music by
Edwin R. Hawkins

Moderately

D7 — **Play 3 times** — G — C/G

mf

G — C/G — G — C/G

Oh hap - py day, ___ (Oh hap - py day) ___ oh hap - py day, ___

G — E7 — A7

(Oh hap - py day) ___ when Je - sus washed, ___

D7 — A7 — D7

oh, ___ when He washed, ___ when Je - sus

A7
D7
G
washed.
He washed the sins a - way.
(Oh hap - py day)
C/G
G
1
C/G
2
D7
Aw hap - py day.
(Oh hap - py day)
Oh hap - py day,
He taught me
G
C/G
how to watch,
joic - ing ev -
G
C/G
fight and pray,
'ry day,
fight and pray,
ev - 'ry day.

G
1
D7
2
C/G
and live re -
Oh hap - py day,
G
C/G
G
oh hap - py day,
(Oh hap - py day)
(Oh hap - py day)
E7
A7
D7
when Je - sus washed,
oh, when He washed,
A7
D7
A7
when Je - sus washed,

D7
G
C/G
He washed my sins a - way.
(Oh, hap - py day)
Oh hap - py day.
G
C/G
G
(Oh hap - py day)
He taught me how
joic -
C/G
G
to watch, fight and pray,
- ing ev - 'ry day,
C/G
G
1
D7
2
C/G
D.S. and Fade
fight and pray,
and live re -
ev - 'ry day.
Oh hap-py day,

Ooo Baby Baby

Words and Music by
William "Smokey" Robinson and Warren Moore

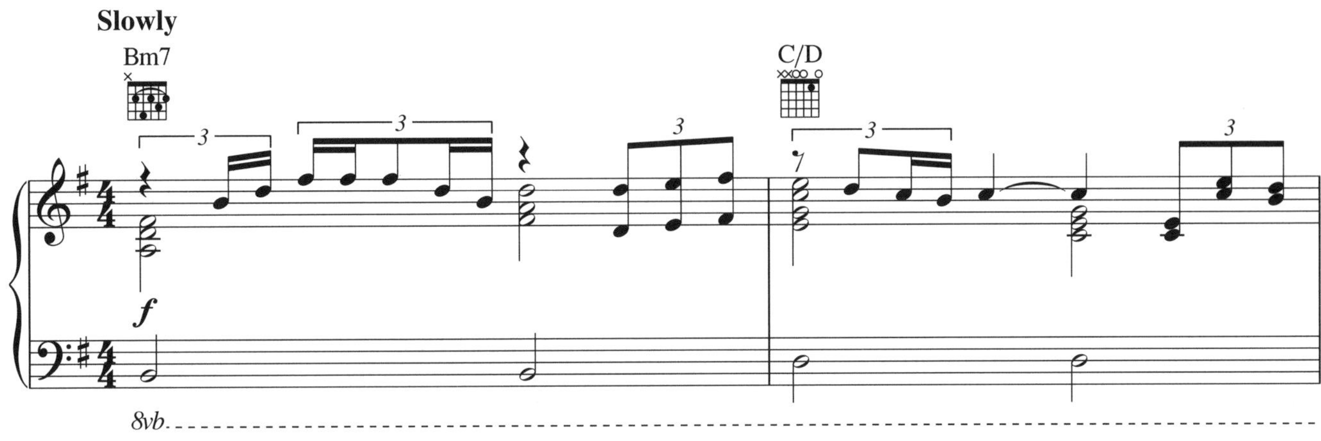

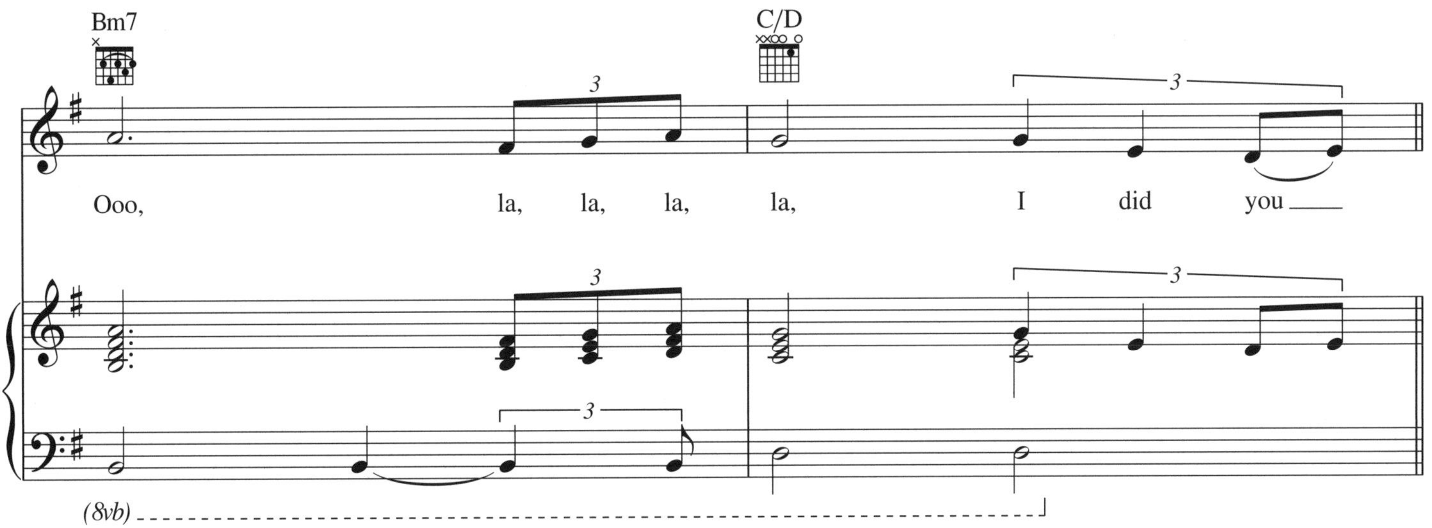

Bm7
Am7
lost you. What a price to pay!
hu - man; you've made mis - takes, too!
I'm
D7
Gmaj7
cry - in'. Ooo, ba - by,
Am7
Gmaj7
ba - by. Ooo, ba - by,
1
Am7
ba - by. Mis -
2, 3
Am7
ba - by. Ooo,

Gmaj7
Am7
Ooo,
ba - by, ba - by.
ba - by, ba - by. Ooo,
Gmaj7
To Coda
Am7
Ooo,
ba - by, ba - by, I'm just a -
ooo,
ba - by,
Bm7
D11
5fr
bout at the end of my rope. But I can't stop

Bm7
D11
5fr
try - in', I can't give up hope 'cause I feel
G
Am7
some - day I'll hold you near. Whis - per I still
Bm7
Am7
D.S. al Coda
(take 2nd ending)
love you un - til that day is here. Ooo, I'm
CODA
Am7
Gmaj9
ba - by. Ooo.
rit.

Red, Red Wine

Words and Music by
Neil Diamond

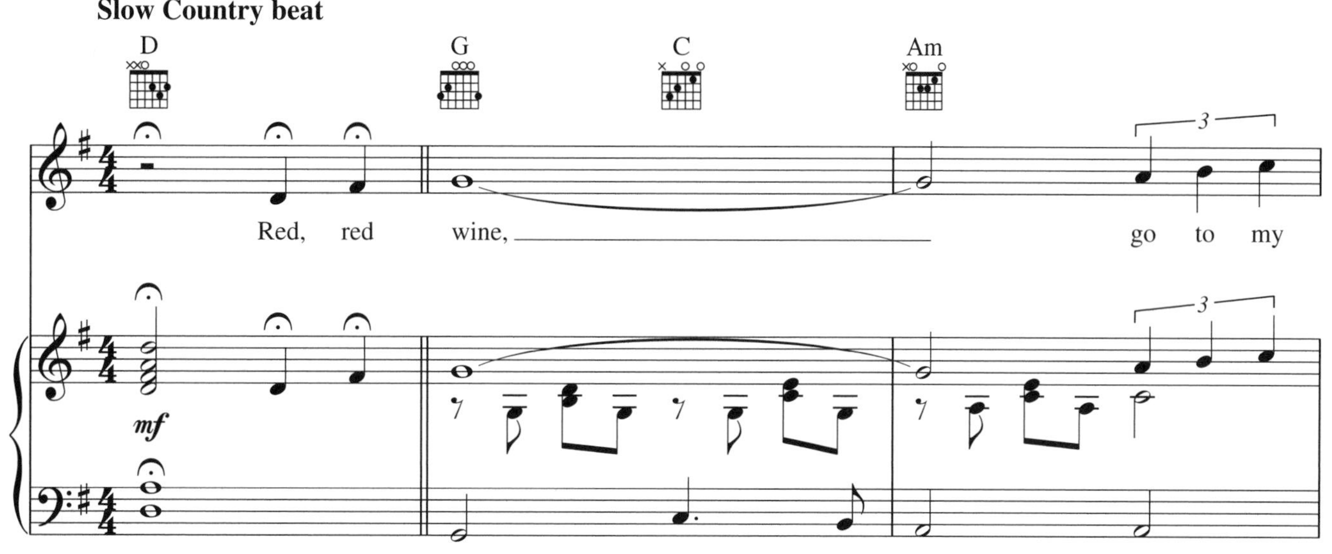

G
C
Am
G
wine, it's up to you.
C
G
C
All I can do, I've done; but mem - 'ries won't
G
C
G
go. No, mem - 'ries won't go.
D
G
I'd have thought that with time thoughts of

C
G
her would leave my head. I was
D
G
wrong, and I find just one
C
Em7/B
Am7
C/G
D
thing makes me for - get. Red, red
G
C
Am
wine, stay close to
3

G
C
me.
Don't let me
be a - lone;
it's tear - ing a -
part
my blue, blue
rit.
heart.
a tempo
Am
C
G/B
Am7
3

Runaround Sue

Words and Music by
Ernie Marasca and Dion Di Mucci

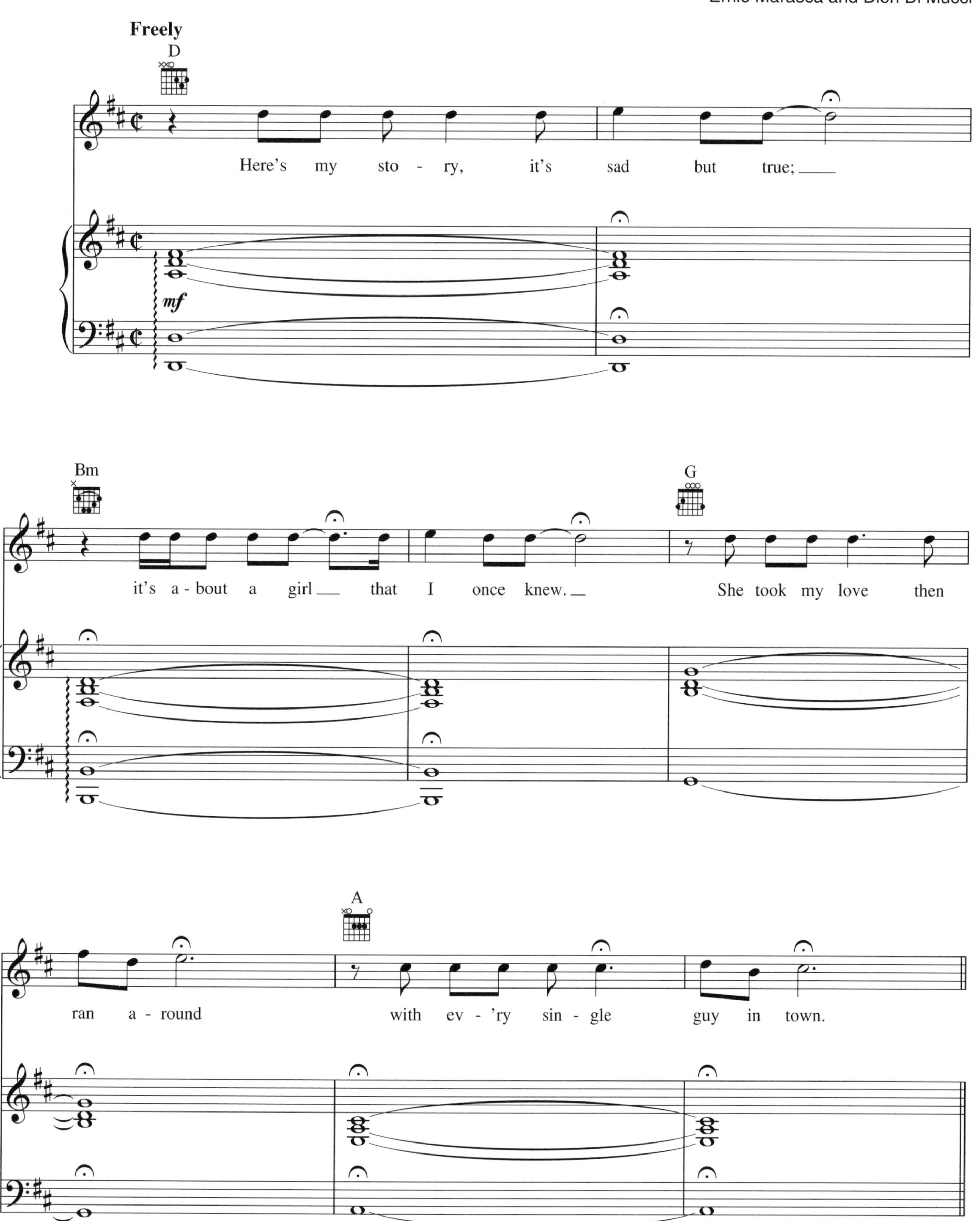

Moderately, with strong off-beat
D
Bm
Hayp hayp bum - da ha - dy ha - dy, hayp hayp
G
bum - da ha - dy ha - dy, hayp hayp bum - da ha - dy ha - dy
1
A
hayp.
2
A
hayp. Ah
D
Bm
I should - a known it from the ver - y start, this girl will leave me with a
I miss her lips and the smile on her face, the touch of her hair and this

G
bro - ken heart. Now lis - ten, peo - ple, what I'm tell - in' you,
girl's warm em - brace. So if you don't wan - na cry like I do,
A
N.C.
a - keep a - way from - a Run - a - round Sue.
D
Hayp hayp
(Oh,
Bm
bum - da ha - dy ha - dy, hayp hayp bum - da ha - dy ha - dy,
oh, oh, oh,
G
A
hayp hayp bum - da ha - dy ha - dy hayp. Ah
oh, oh.)

G
D
She likes to trav - el a - round.
She'll love you, but she'll put you down.
G
Now, peo - ple, let me put you wise:
A
N.C.
D
Sue goes out with oth - er guys. Here's the mor - al and the sto - ry from the
Bm
guy who knows, I fell in love and my love still grows.

G
A
N.C.
Ask an - y fool that she ev - er knew, _ they'll say keep a - way from - a
D
Run - a - round Sue. Hayp hayp bum - da ha - dy ha - dy,
Bm
G
hayp hayp bum - da ha - dy ha - dy, hayp hayp
A
N.C.
D.S. and Fade
bum - da ha - dy ha - dy hayp. Ah

Runaway

Words and Music by
Del Shannon and Max Crook

C7
Fm
strong.
And as I
E♭
3fr
still walk on, I think of the things we've done to -
D♭
C7
geth - er while our hearts were young.
F
I'm a - walk - in' in the rain.

Dm
F
Tears are fall - in' and I feel a pain, a - wish - in' you were
Dm
here by me to end this mis - er - y. And I
F
Dm
won - der, wo - wo - wo - wo - won - der
F
why, why why why why

Dm
why she ran a - way and I wonder
F
C7
where she will stay,
Bb/C
my lit - tle
F
run - a - way,
Bb
run - run - run - run - run - a - way.
1
C7
2
run - a - way.

Save the Country

Words and Music by
Laura Nyro

C/D
G/D
3fr
I got fu - ry in my soul. Fu - ry's gon - na take me to the
C/D
Bm7
Gmaj7
F♯m7
Em7
G/A
A
glo - ry goal. In my mind, I can't stu - dy war no more.
D
Save the peo - ple.
Save the chil - dren.
Save the coun - try, save the coun - try, now.

D
Em/A
G/A
3fr
Come on peo - ple! Come on chil - dren! Come on down to the
Gmaj7
F#m7
Em7
G
Gsus2
C
glo - ry riv - er. Gon - na wash you up, and wash you down;
Slower
G/B
Am7
A
gon - na lay the dev - il, long lay the dev - il, lay that dev - il down.
rit.

Tempo I
D
G/A
3fr
Gmaj7
Come on peo - ple! Sons and moth - ers! Keep the dream _ of the
F♯m7
Em9
G
two young broth - ers. Gon - na take that dream _ and ride that dove.
C
We _ can build the dream with love, I know. _ We _
Gmaj7/C
could build a dream with love, _ I know. _ We _ could build a dream with love, _

F♯m7
Gmaj7/C
F♯m7
chil - dren. We could build the dream with love. Oh, peo - ple, we
G
F♯m7
Gmaj7/C
could build a dream with love, I know. We could build a dream with love.
Slightly faster
F♯m7
C/D
G
D
C/D
D
C/D
I got fu - ry, I got fu - ry, I got fu - ry,
C
G/D
D
C/D
I got fu - ry in my soul. Gon - na take me to the
rit.

Tempo I
Bm7
Gmaj7
F♯m7
Em7
G/A
A
3fr
glo - ry goal. In my mind, I can't stu - dy war no more.
Faster
D
G/D
C/D
Save the peo - ple.
Save the chil - dren.
Save the coun - try.
Ev - 'ry - bod - y,
C
C/B
C/A
save the coun - try, save the coun - try, save the coun - try.
accel.

Very lively
Em/F
D
G/D
C/D
C
G
G/F♯
Asus4
1.
2.
3fr
Save the coun - try.
*Yeah!
Save the peo - ple.
Save the chil - dren.
Save the coun - try.
Come on down to the glo - ry riv - er.
Come on down to the glo - ry riv - er.
*Sing 1st time only.

D
G/D
C/D
3fr
Save the peo - ple.
Save the chil - dren.
Save the coun - try.
Yeah!
F/D
f
Repeat ad lib
Last time
Cmaj7
N.C.

Save the Last Dance for Me

Words and Music by
Doc Pomus and Mort Shuman

B♭7
E♭7
A♭
4fr
Just don't for - get who's tak - ing you home and in whose arms you're
E♭
3fr
B♭7
gon - na be.
So, dar - lin', save the
1
E♭
3fr
2
E♭
3fr
last dance for me.
Oh, I
me.
N.C.
B♭7
Ba - by, don't you know I love you so?
Can't you feel it when we

E♭
3fr
N.C.
B♭7
touch? I will nev - er, nev - er let you go.
E♭
3fr
I love you, oh, so much. You can
dance, go and car - ry on till the night is gone till it's
B♭7
time to go. If {he / she} asks if you're

E♭
3fr
all a - lone, can {he she} take you home, you've got to tell {him her} no.
B♭7
E♭7
A♭
4fr
'Cause don't for - get who's tak - ing you home and in whose arms you're
E♭
3fr
B♭7
gon - na be. So, dar - lin', save the last dance for
1
E♭
3fr
2
E♭
3fr
me. You can me.

Shout

Words and Music by O'Kelly Isley,
Ronald Isley and Rudolph Isley

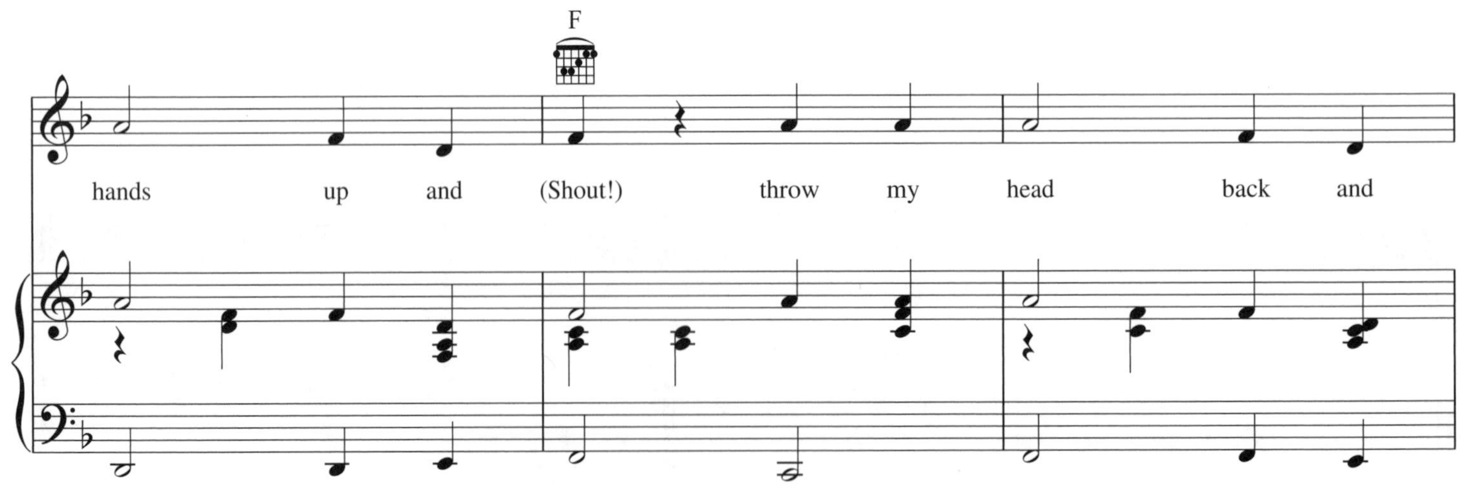

Dm
F
(Shout!) come on, now. Don't for - get to
(Shout!)
Dm
say you will.
F
Dm
Don't for - get to say yeah, yeah, yeah,
F
yeah, yeah. Say you

Dm
F
will. Say it right now ba - by. Say
Dm
you will. Come on, come on.
F
Dm
Say you will hey, hey, hey.
F
Dm
Say you will. Come on now.

F
Dm
(Say) Say that you love me. (Say) Say that you
(Say) Say that you want me. (Say) You wan - na
need me.
please me.
(Say) Come on, now.
(Say) Come on, now. (Say) Come on, now.
N.C.
(Say.) I still re - mem - ber
(Shoo - by

when you used to be nine years old
doo - wop.)
Dm
yeah, yeah.
(Shoo - by - doo.)
F
I was a fool for you from the
Dm
bot - tom of my soul, yeah.

F
Now that you've grown up
Dm
you're old e - nough to know,
yeah, yeah. You wan - na leave
F
me. You wan - na
(Shoo - by doo - wop.)

Dm
let me go.
(Shoo - by doo - wop, doo -
Swing
N.C.
F7
I want you to know.
wop.)
I said I want you to know
right now, yeah. You've been good to me ba - by,
bet - ter than I've been to my - self, yeah, hey. And if you ev - er

leave me I don't want no - bod - y else, hey, hey.
I said I want you to know, hey. I said I want you to know
right now, yeah, yeah. You know you make me wan - na
Original Tempo
F
Dm
Play 7 times
(Shout!)
(w/lead vocal ad libs.)
(Shout!)

F
N.C.
Freely
F
(Shout!)
Now wait a min - ute. I feel
B♭/F
F
B♭/F
F
all right.
(Yeah, yeah, yeah, yeah, yeah,
F7
Now that I've got my wom - an, I feel all
yeah.)
B♭7
right.
Ev - 'ry time I think a - bout you. You been so good to me.
(Yeah, yeah, yeah, yeah, yeah.)

Original Tempo
F
You know you make me wan - na (Shout!) lift my
Dm
hands up and (Shout!) Throw my head back and
F
Dm
(Shout!) pick my hands up and (Shout!) Come on
F
now. (Shout!) Take it eas - y.

Dm
F
(Shout!) Take it eas - y. (Shout!) Take it eas - - y.
Dm
(Shout!) A lit - tle bit soft - er now.
F
Dm
(Shout!) A lit - tle bit soft - er now. (Shout!) A lit - tle bit
decresc.
soft - er now.
Play 8 times
F
(Shout!) A lit - tle bit loud - er now.
cresc.

Dm
Play 6 times
F
(Shout!) A lit - tle bit loud - er now.
(Shout!) Hey,
Dm
F
hey. (Hey, hey.) Hey,
Dm
hey. (Hey, hey.)
F
Dm
Hey. (Hey.)

F
Dm
Hey.
(Hey.)
F
Dm
Shout now.
Jump up and shout now.
Jump up and shout now.
F
Jump up and
Dm
F
shout now.
Ev - 'ry - bod - y shout now.

Dm
Ev - 'ry - bod - y shout now. Ev - 'ry - bod - y
F
Dm
shout, shout, shout, shout, shout, shout,
Repeat and Fade
F
shout, shout. Shout, shout, shout, shout.
Dm
Optional Ending
F
Shout, shout, shout, shout. Shout.

Son-of-a-Preacher Man

Words and Music by
John Hurley and Ronnie Wilkins

we'd go walk - in'. And then he'd look in - to my eyes,
thing is al - right, and "Can I sneak a - way a - gain to - night?"
Lord knows, to my sur - prise:
C
The on - ly one who could ev - er reach me
F
C
was the son - of - a - preach - er man. The on - ly boy who could ev - er teach me
F
C
G7
was the son - of - a - preach - er man, yes he was, he was.

F
1
C
Ooh.
2
B♭
How well I re - mem - ber
F
the look that was in his eyes. __ Steal - in' kiss - es from me on the sly,
G7
tak - in' time to make time, tell - in' me that he's all mine. ___

C7
Learn-in' from each oth - er knowin' and look-in' to see how much we've grown. And the
F
Bb
F
on - ly one who could ev - er reach me was the son-of-a-preach-er man. The
Bb
F
on - ly one who could ev - er teach me was the son-of-a-preach-er man; yes, he was.
C7
Repeat and Fade
Bb
Optional Ending
F
Yeah! The

Spanish Harlem

Words and Music by
Jerry Leiber and Phil Spector

F
It is a spec - ial one it's nev - er
With eyes as black as coal that look down
seen the sun. It on - ly comes out when the moon is on the
in my soul, and start a fire there and then I lose con -
C
run and all the stars are gleam - ing.
trol, I have to beg your par - don.
G
It's grow - ing in the street right up
I'm going to pick that rose and watch

1
C
thru the con - crete but soft and sweet _ and dream - ing. _
2
C
her as she grows _ in my gar - den. _

Stand by Me

Words and Music by
Jerry Leiber, Mike Stoller
and Ben E. King

F
see, oh, I won't be a - fraid,
sea, I won't cry, I won't cry,
Dm C Dm
no, I won't be a - fraid
no, I won't shed a tear
just as
B♭ C F
long as you stand, stand by me.
So dar - ling, dar - ling,
Dm C Dm
stand by me, stand by me, oh

B♭
C
C7
F
stand,
stand by me,
stand by me.
1
2
If the
Dar-ling,
stand
by me,
Dm
C
Dm
B♭
stand by me,
oh
stand,
C
C7
F
Repeat and Fade
stand by me,
stand by me.
When-ev-er I'm in trou-ble, won't you

Tell Laura I Love Her

Words and Music by
Jeff Barry and Ben Raleigh

Moderately

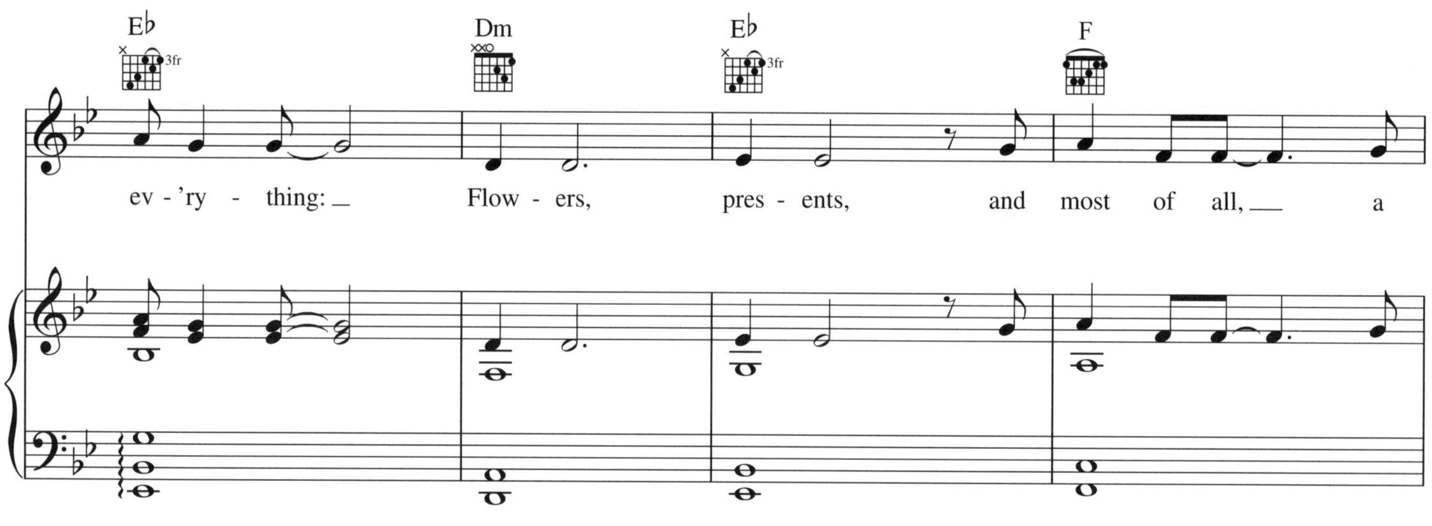

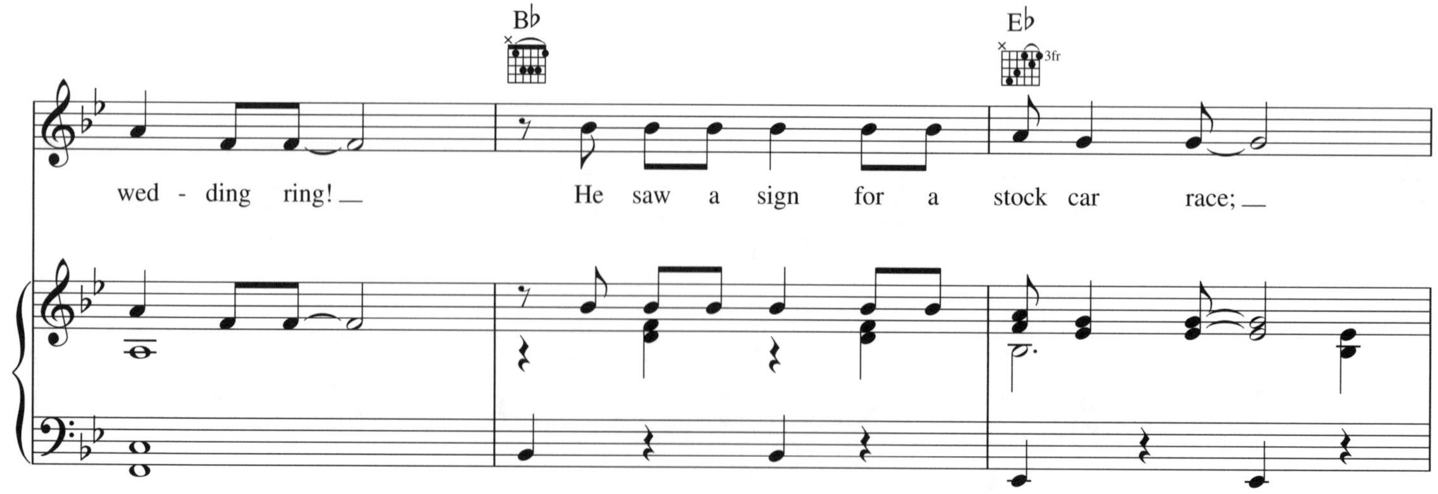

B♭
E♭
3fr
Dm
a thou-sand dol-lar prize, it read. He could-n't get Lau-ra
E♭
3fr
F
on the phone, so to her moth-er Tom-my said:
B♭
3
"Tell Lau-ra I love her! Tell Lau-ra I
Cm
3fr
B♭
E♭6
need her! Tell Lau-ra I may be late, I've some-thing to do

F7
B♭
that can - not wait."
E♭
3fr
He drove his car to the rac - ing grounds;
he was the young-est
E♭
Dm
driv - er there.
The crowd roared as they start - ed the race; 'round the
3
F
track they drove at a dead - ly pace!
No one knows what

E♭
B♭
E♭
hap-pened that day, how his car o - ver - turned in flames, but
Dm
E♭
F
as they pulled him from the twist - ed wreck, with his dy - ing breath, they
B♭
heard him say: "Tell Lau - ra I love her!
Cm
B♭
Tell Lau - ra I need her! Tell Lau - ra not to cry, my

E♭6
F7
B♭
To Coda
love for her will nev - er die!"
E♭
B♭
Now, in the chap - el Lau - ra prays
for her Tom - my who
E♭
Dm
E♭
passed a - way. It was just for Lau - ra he lived and died; a -
F
D.S. al Coda
lone in the chap - el she can hear him cry:
CODA
3fr

These Eyes

Written by
Burton Cummings and Randy Bachman

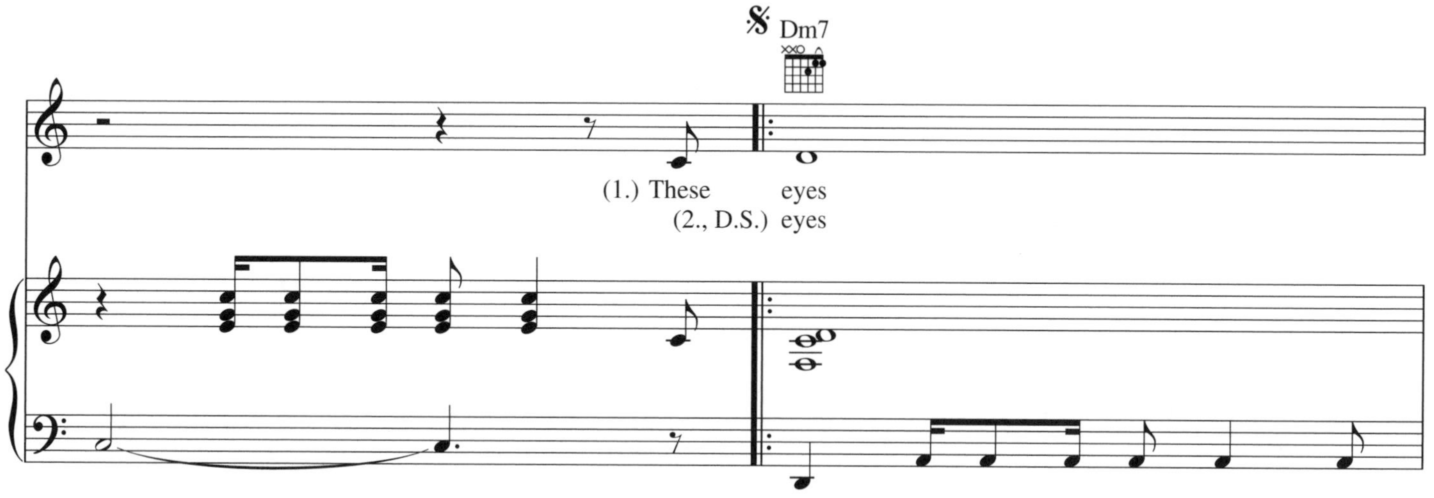

Dm7
Cmaj7
arms long to hold you a-
heart could not ac-cept and pre-
C
Am
C
gain. The hurt-in's on me,
tend. The hurt-in's on me,
Am
C
Am
but I will nev-er be free.
but I will nev-er be free.
You gave a prom-ise to me
You took the vow with me
C
G
To Coda
1
and you broke it, and you broke it. These
when you spoke it, when you spoke

2
G7sus
Cmaj7
G7sus
it.
These eyes
Cmaj7
G7sus
Cmaj7
are cry - in'. These eyes have seen a lot of love, but they're nev - er gon - na see an - oth - er
D
Dmaj7
A7sus
one like I had with you.
These eyes
Dmaj7
A7sus
Dmaj7
are cry - in' These eyes have seen a lot of love, but they're nev - er gon - na see an - oth - er

E
one like I had with you.
Emaj7
B7sus
2fr
Emaj7
B7sus
2fr
These eyes are cry - in'. These eyes have
Emaj7
seen a lot of love, but they're nev - er gon - na see an - oth - er one like I had with
F#
G
D.S. al Coda
you. These
CODA
C
C(add9)
it.

Those Were the Days

Words and Music by
Gene Raskin

B
B9
E
dreamed of all the great things we would do.
smile at one an - oth - er and we'd say.
Was that lone - ly fel - low real - ly me?
in our hearts the dreams are still the same.
Those were the
Moderately
Am
Dm
days, my friend. We thought they'd nev - er end. We'd sing and
G
G7
C
dance for - ev - er and a day; we'd live the
Dm
Am
life we chose, we'd fight and nev - er lose, for we were

E7
Am
young and sure to have our way.
A
Dm
La la la la la la la la la la la la
F7
E7
those were the days, oh yes, those were the
1-3
Am
days.
4
Am
days.

To Sir, with Love

from TO SIR, WITH LOVE

Words by Don Black

Music by Marc London

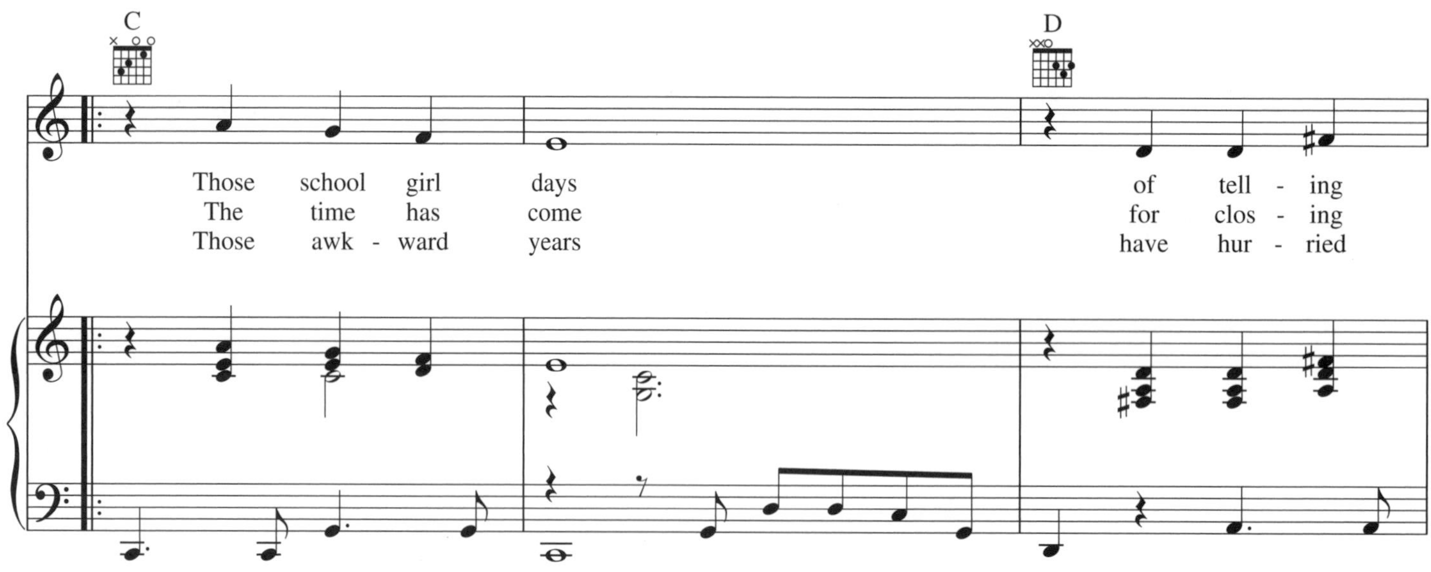

D
but in my mind I know they
And as I leave, I know that
Why is it, sir, chil - dren grow
F
C
will still live on and on.
I am leav - ing my best friend.
up to be peo - ple one day?
B7
Em
But how do you thank some - one who has
A friend who taught me right from wrong and
What takes the place of climb - ing trees and
B7
Em
D
tak - en you from cray - ons to per - fume. It is - n't
weak from strong, that's a lot to learn. What can I
dirt - y knees in the world out - side? What is there

G
D
A7
eas - y but I'll try. If you
give you in re - turn? If you
for you I can buy? If you
D
C/D
D
want - ed the sky I'd write a - cross the sky in let - ters that would
want - ed the moon I would try to make a start, but
want - ed the world I'd sur - round it with a wall; I'd scrawl these
C/D
D
G
soar a thou - sand feet high "To sir, with
I would rath - er you let me give my heart to sir, with
words with let - ters ten feet tall: "To sir, with
1, 2
A7
C6
Dm7
G7
love."
love.
3
A7
D
D6/9
4fr
love."

The Tracks of My Tears

Words and Music by
William "Smokey" Robinson, Warren Moore
and Marvin Tarplin

C
D
might be laugh - in' loud and heart - y,
may be cute, she's just a sub - sti - tute be - cause
G
C
G
Am7
G
G
C
deep in - side I'm blue.
you're the per - ma - nent one.
So take a good look at my
D
G
C
D
face. You'll see my smile looks out of place.
If you look
Look a lit - tle bit
G
C
D
G
C
clos - er
clos - er,
it's eas - y to trace the tracks of my tears.

G Am7 G
C G
1 C G
I need you, need you.
2 C G
N.C.
C G
you.
Hey, hey,
C G
C G
C G
yeah. (Out - side.) I'm mas-quer - ad - ing, (In -
C G
C G
C G
side,) my hope is fad - ing, (just a clown.) ooh yeah, since you

C G F♯m Em G F♯m Em G F♯m Em G F♯m7 Em
put me down. My smile is my make-up I wear since my break-up with
D G C D
you. Ba-by, take a good look at my face. You'll see my
G C D G C
smile looks out of place. Yeah, just look clos-er, it's eas-y to
Repeat and Fade
D G C G Am7 G D
trace the tracks of my tears, ba-by, ba-by, ba-by, ba-by. Take a

Under the Boardwalk

Words and Music by
Artie Resnick and Kenny Young

G
tired feet were fire - proof,
dogs and french fries they sell.
End instrumental
(1.) Un - der the board -
(2., 3.) Un - der the board -
C
- walk,
- walk,
G
down by the sea,
down by the sea,
yeah, on a blan - ket with my ba - by's
yeah, on a blan - ket with my ba - by's
D7
where I'll
where I'll
G
be.
be.
Em
(Un - der the board - walk,) out

D
of the sun,
(un - der the board - walk,)
we'll be hav - in' some fun.
(Un - der the
Em
D
peo - ple walk - in' a - bove,
board - walk,)
(un - der the board - walk,)
we'll be
Em
1, 2
3
fall - in' in love un - der the board - walk, board - walk.
(un - der the board - walk, board - walk.)
From the
Instrumental
walk.
walk.)

Up on the Roof

Words and Music by
Gerry Goffin and Carole King

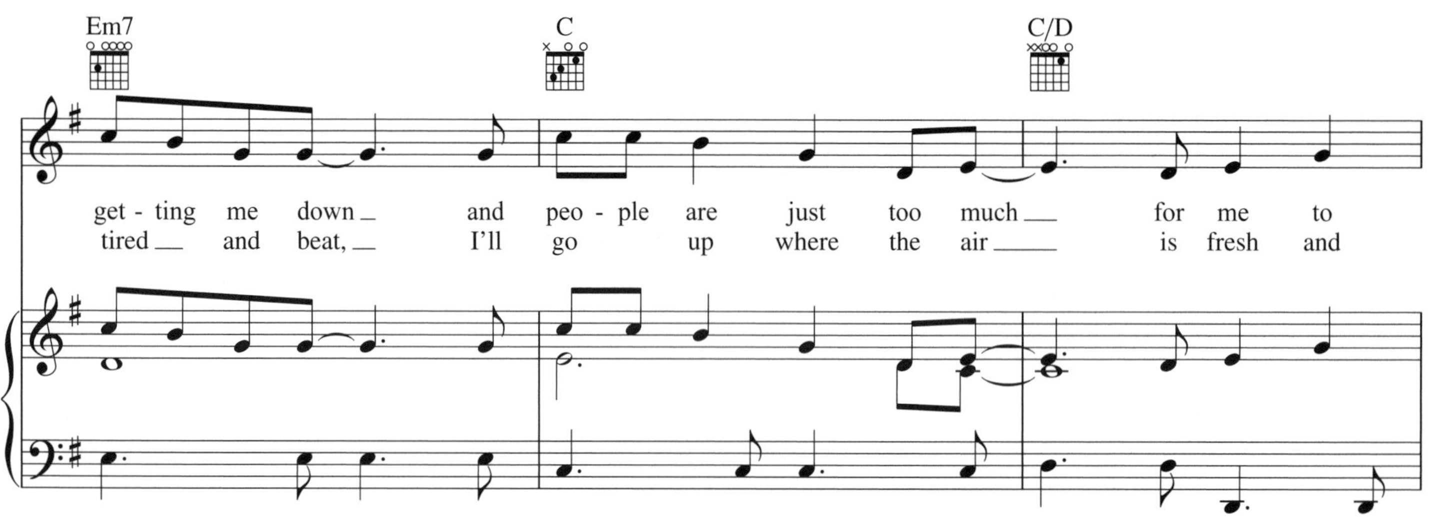

Em7
C
C/D
top of the stairs and all my cares just drift right in - to space.
hus - tling crowds and all that rat - race noise down in the street.
G
C
On the roof it's the
On the roof that's the
C6
Cmaj7
C6
peace - ful as can be and
on - ly place I know where
G
Em7
C
there the world be - low don't both - er me.
you just have to wish to make it so;

1
Am7/D
2
Am7/D
G
So, when up on the roof.
Em7
C
C/D
G
C
C6
Cmaj7
At night the stars put on a show for free,
C6
G
Em7
and, dar - ling, you can share it all with

C
Am7/D
N.C.
G
me.
I keep a - tell - in' you right smack dab in the
Em7
C
C/D
mid - dle of town I found a par - a - dise that's trou - ble
G
Em7
proof.
And if this world starts get - tin' you down, there's
C
C/D
G
room e - nough for two up on the roof.
rit.

Walk Like a Man

Words and Music by
Bob Crewe and Bob Gaudio

C/G G D7
like a man.
G Am G Am
Oh, how you tried to cut me down to size,
Bye - yi, ba - by, I don't mean may - be;
G Am G Am
tell - in' dirt - y lies to your friends. But,
gon - na get a - long some - how.
G Am G Am
my own fa - ther said, "Give her up, don't both - er, the
Soon you'll be cry - ing, on ac - count of all your ly - ing. Oh

G Am G N.C. C C/E F
world is - n't com - ing to an end." He said it. "Walk like a man,
yeah, just look who's laugh - ing now. I'm gon - na walk like a man,
C F C Em F G
talk like a man, walk like a man, my son.
fast as I can, walk like a man from you.
C C/E F C F
No wom - an's worth crawl - in' on the earth, so,
I'll tell the world for - get a - bout it, girl, and
C Em 1 F D 2 F D
walk like a man, my son."
walk like a man from you.

G
C
Ooh
(walk,
walk,
walk,
walk)
Repeat and Fade
Optional Ending
ooh.)

What a Wonderful World

Words and Music by
George David Weiss and Bob Thiele

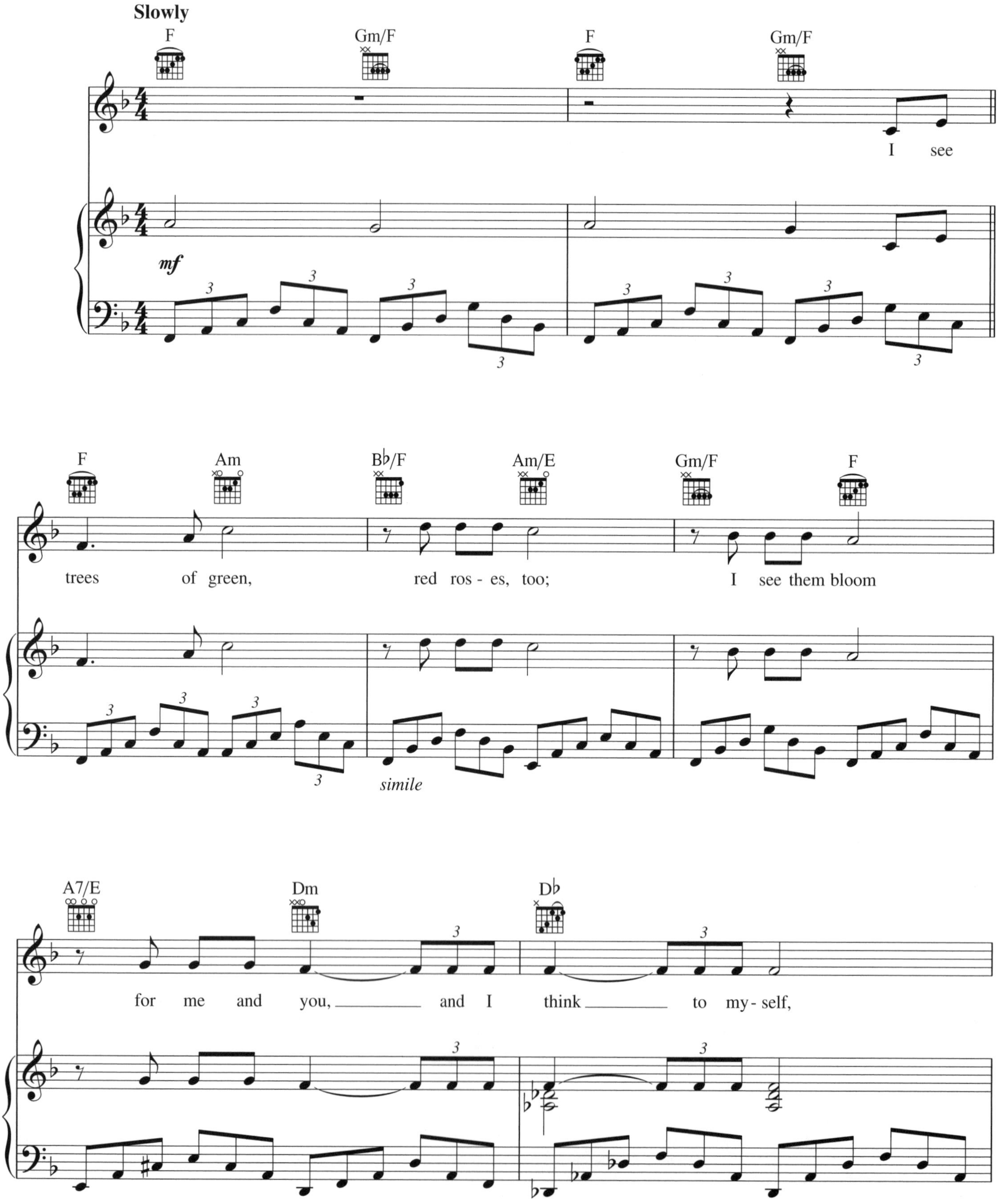

Slowly

F Gm/F F Gm/F

mf

I see

F Am B♭/F Am/E Gm/F F

trees of green, red ros - es, too; I see them bloom

simile

C11 C7 F F+ B♭maj7/F C7
"What a won - der - ful world." I see
F Am B♭/F Am Gm7 F
skies of blue and clouds of white, the bright blessed day, the
A7 Dm D♭
dark sa - cred night, and I think to my - self,
C11 C7 F B♭/F F
"What a won - der - ful world." The

C7
F
colors of the rain - bow, so pret - ty in the sky, are
C7
F
al - so on the fac - es of peo - ple go - in' by. I see
Dm
C/E
Dm/F
C/G
friends shak - in' hands, say - in', "How do you do?"
3
Dm/F
F♯dim
Gm7
F♯dim
C/G
C7
They're real - ly say - in', "I love you." I hear
cresc.
f
9fr

F
Am
B♭/F
Am/E
Gm/F
F
ba - bies cry, I watch them grow; they'll learn much more than
simile
A7/E
Dm
D♭
C11
C7
I'll ever know, and I think to my-self, "What a won - der - ful
F
Am7♭5
D7
Rubato
Gm7
world." Yes, I think to my - self,
C7♭9
F
Gm/F
F
"What a won - der - ful world."
rit.

A Whiter Shade of Pale

Words and Music by
Keith Reid, Gary Brooker
and Matthew Fisher

F
F/E
Dm7
turned cart - wheels 'cross the floor;
though in truth we were at sea.
and the truth is plain to see."
G
G/F
Em
G7
I was feel - ing kind of sea - sick,
So I took her by the look - ing glass
But I wan - dered through my play - ing cards
C
C/B
Am
Em
the crowd called out for more.
and forced her to a - gree,
and would not let her be
F
Dm/E
Dm7
The room was hum - ming hard - er
say - ing, "You must be the mer - maid
one of six - teen ves - tal vir - gins

G
G/F
Em
G7
as the ceil - ing flew a - way.
who took Nep - tune for a ride."
who were leav - ing for the coast.
C
C/B
Am
Em
When we called out for an - oth - er drink
But she smiled at me so sad - ly
And al-though my eyes were o - pen,
F
Dm/E
Dm7
Em/G
the wait - er brought a tray.
that my an - ger straight - way died.
they might just as well been closed.
And so it
C6
C/B
Am
C
was that lat - er

F
F/E
Dm7
as the mill - er told his tale,
G
G/F
Em
G7
that her face at first just ghostly turned a
C
F
To Coda
1
C
G7
whit - er shade of pale.
2
C
G7
D.C. al Coda
pale.
CODA
C
pale.

Winchester Cathedral

Words and Music by
Geoff Stephens

G7
- thing but you did-n't try.
You did-n't do noth-
C
C7
2fr
- ing; you let her walk by.
Now ev-'ry-one knows
just how much I need-ed that girl.
F
D7
She would-n't have gone far a - way,
if on-ly you'd

N.C.
G7
C
start - ed ring-ing your bell.
Win - ches - ter Ca - the - dral,
G7
you're bring - ing me down.
You stood and you watched
C
1
2
as
my ba - by left town.
town.
C
G13
C
sfz

You've Lost That Lovin' Feelin'

Words and Music by
Barry Mann, Cynthia Weil
and Phil Spector

C
Dm7
You're try - ing hard not to show it,
It makes me just feel like cry - ing,
Em7
Fmaj7
F/G
G
but, ba - by, ba - by, I know it.
'cause, ba - by, some - thing beau - ti - ful's dy - ing.
(Ba - by)
C
Dm/C
G7
You've lost that lov - in' feel - in', whoa oh, that lov -
C
Dm/C
- in' feel - in'. You've lost that lov - in' feel - in'! Now it's

B♭/C
gone, gone, gone, whoa oh oh oh.
1
C
Now, there's no
2
C
F
G
F
G
C
F
G
F
G
C
F
Ba - by, ba - by, I'd get down on my knees for you.
G
F
G
C
F
G
F
G
If that would make you love me like you used to

C F G F G
do.
C F G F G
We had a love, a love, a love you don't find ev - 'ry
C F G F G C F
day. So don't, don't,
G F G C F G F G
don't, don't let it slip a - way.

C
F
G
F
G
Ba - by,
ba - by,
I beg you
(Ba - by,)
(ba - by,)
please,
(beg you please,)
please,
I need your
(please,)
love,
I need your
love,
so bring it on
(I need your love,)
(I need your love,)
back,
so bring it on
back.
(bring it on back,)
(Bring it on back.)

C
Dm/C
G7
Bring back that lov - in' feel - in', whoa oh, that lov -
- in' feel - in'.
Dm/C
Bring back that lov - in' feel - in', 'cause it's
B♭/C
gone, gone, gone, and I can't go
C
Repeat and Fade
on, whoa oh oh oh.

Young Girl

Words and Music by
Jerry Fuller

Cm7
Bbmaj7
Cm7
charms of a wom - an,
per - fume and make - up,
home to your ma - ma,
Bbmaj7
Cm7
Bbmaj7
you've kept the se - cret of your youth.
you're just a ba - by in dis - guise.
I'm sure she won - ders where you are.
Cm7
F7
D7
You led me to be - lieve you're
And though you know that it is
Get out of here be - fore I
Gm
C7
Bb
old e - nough to give me love and now it
wrong to be a - lone with me, that come - on
have the time to change my mind, 'cause I'm a -

F7
G♭
1, 2
B♭7
hurts to know the truth.
look is in your eyes.
fraid we'll go too far.
Oh.
Oh.
3
B♭7
Oh.
E♭
3fr
Dm
Young girl, get out of my mind,
E♭
3fr
Dm
Cm7
3fr
my love for you is way out of line. Bet - ter run, girl,
F7
A♭
4fr
G♭
Repeat and Fade
you're much too young, girl.

Yummy, Yummy, Yummy

Words and Music by
Arthur Resnick and Joe Levine

E♭
F
B♭
just a - what I'm gon - na do.
love is like peach - es and cream.
sweet thing, that ain't no lie.
Ooh, love to hold ya, ooh,
Kind - a like sug - ar, kind -
I love to hold ya, ooh,
F
love to kiss ya, ooh, love, I love it so.
- a like spic - es, kind - a like, like what you do.
love to kiss ya, ooh, love, I love it so.
F9
B♭
Ooh, love, you're sweet - er, sweet - er than sug - ar. Ooh,
Kind - a sounds fun - ny, but love, hon - ey, hon -
Ooh, love, you're sweet - er, sweet - er than sug - ar. Ooh,

F
E♭
3fr
To Coda
love, I won't let you go.
- ey, I love you.
love, I won't let you go.
1
F
2
B♭
F
B♭
Ba da, ba da da da da. Ba da da da da, ba da da da da.
F
D.S. al Coda
CODA
B♭
F
Repeat ad lib. and Fade
Ba da, da, ba da da da da. Ba da da da

More Great Piano/Vocal Books

FROM CHERRY LANE

For a complete listing of Cherry Lane titles available, including contents listings, please visit our web site at
www.cherrylane.com

02501590 Sara Bareilles – Kaleidoscope Heart $17.99
02501136 Sara Bareilles – Little Voice $16.95
00102353 Sara Bareilles – Once Upon Another Time $12.99
02501505 The Black Eyed Peas – The E.N.D. $19.99
02502171 The Best of Boston $17.95
02501614 Zac Brown Band – The Foundation $19.99
02501618 Zac Brown Band – You Get What You Give $19.99
02501123 Buffy the Vampire Slayer – Once More with Feeling $18.95
02500665 Sammy Cahn Songbook $24.95
02501688 Colbie Caillat – All of You $17.99
02501454 Colbie Caillat – Breakthrough $17.99
02501127 Colbie Caillat – Coco $16.95
02500838 Best of Joe Cocker $16.95
02502165 John Denver Anthology – Revised $22.95
02500002 John Denver Christmas $14.95
02502166 John Denver's Greatest Hits $17.95
02502151 John Denver – A Legacy in Song (Softcover) $24.95
02500566 Poems, Prayers and Promises: The Art and Soul of John Denver $19.95
02500326 John Denver – The Wildlife Concert $17.95
02500501 John Denver and the Muppets: A Christmas Together $9.95
02501186 The Dresden Dolls – The Virginia Companion $39.95
02509922 The Songs of Bob Dylan $29.95
02500497 Linda Eder – Gold $14.95
02500396 Linda Eder – Christmas Stays the Same $17.95
02502209 Linda Eder – It's Time $17.95
02501542 Foreigner – The Collection $19.99
02500535 Erroll Garner Anthology $19.95
02500318 Gladiator $12.95
02502126 Best of Guns N' Roses $17.95
02502072 Guns N' Roses – Selections from Use Your Illusion I and II $17.95
02500014 Sir Roland Hanna Collection $19.95
02501447 Eric Hutchinson – Sounds Like This $17.99
02500856 Jack Johnson – Anthology $19.95
02501140 Jack Johnson – Sleep Through the Static $16.95
02501564 Jack Johnson – To the Sea $19.99
02501546 Jack's Mannequin – *The Glass Passenger* and *The Dear Jack EP* $19.99
02500834 The Best of Rickie Lee Jones $16.95
02500381 Lenny Kravitz – Greatest Hits $14.95
02501318 John Legend – Evolver $19.99
02500822 John Legend – Get Lifted $16.99
02503701 Man of La Mancha $11.95
02501047 Dave Matthews Band – Anthology $24.95
02502192 Dave Matthews Band – Under the Table and Dreaming $17.95
02501514 John Mayer Anthology – Volume 1 $22.99
02501504 John Mayer – Battle Studies $19.99
02500987 John Mayer – Continuum $16.95
02500681 John Mayer – Heavier Things $16.95
02500563 John Mayer – Room for Squares $16.95
02500081 Natalie Merchant – Ophelia $14.95
02502446 Jason Mraz – Love Is a Four Letter Word $19.99
02500863 Jason Mraz – Mr. A-Z $17.95
02501467 Jason Mraz – We Sing. We Dance. We Steal Things. $19.99
02502895 Nine $17.95
02501411 Nine – Film Selections $19.99
02500425 Time and Love: The Art and Soul of Laura Nyro $21.99
02502204 The Best of Metallica $17.95
02501497 Ingrid Michaelson – Everybody $17.99
02501496 Ingrid Michaelson – Girls and Boys $19.99
02501768 Ingrid Michaelson – Human Again $17.99
02501529 Monte Montgomery Collection $24.99
02500857 Anna Nalick – Wreck of the Day $16.95
02501336 Amanda Palmer – Who Killed Amanda Palmer? $17.99
02501004 Best of Gram Parsons $16.95
02500010 Tom Paxton – The Honor of Your Company $17.95
02507962 Peter, Paul & Mary – Holiday Concert $17.95
02500145 Pokemon 2.B.A. Master $12.95
02500026 The Prince of Egypt $16.95
02500660 Best of Bonnie Raitt $17.95
02502189 The Bonnie Raitt Collection $22.95
02502088 Bonnie Raitt – Luck of the Draw $14.95
02507958 Bonnie Raitt – Nick of Time $14.95
02502218 Kenny Rogers – The Gift $16.95
02501577 She & Him – Volume One $16.99
02501578 She & Him – Volume Two $16.99
02500414 Shrek $16.99
02500536 Spirit – Stallion of the Cimarron $16.95
02500166 Steely Dan – Anthology $17.95
02500622 Steely Dan – Everything Must Go $14.95
02500284 Steely Dan – Two Against Nature $14.95
02500344 Billy Strayhorn: An American Master $17.95
02500515 Barbra Streisand – Christmas Memories $16.95
02502164 Barbra Streisand – The Concert $22.95
02500550 Essential Barbra Streisand $24.95
02502228 Barbra Streisand – Higher Ground $17.99
02501065 Barbra Streisand – Live in Concert 2006 $19.95
02501485 Barbra Streisand – Love Is the Answer $19.99
02501722 Barbra Streisand – What Matters Most $19.99
02502178 The John Tesh Collection $17.95
02503623 John Tesh – A Family Christmas $15.95
02503630 John Tesh – Grand Passion $16.95
02500307 John Tesh – Pure Movies 2 $16.95
02501068 The Evolution of Robin Thicke $19.95
02500565 Thoroughly Modern Millie $17.99
02501399 Best of Toto $19.99
02502175 Tower of Power – Silver Anniversary $17.95
02501403 Keith Urban – Defying Gravity $17.99
02501008 Keith Urban – Love, Pain & The Whole Crazy Thing $17.95
02501141 Keith Urban – Greatest Hits $16.99
02502198 The "Weird Al" Yankovic Anthology $17.95
02500334 Maury Yeston – December Songs $17.95
02502225 The Maury Yeston Songbook $19.95

See your local music dealer or contact:

7777 W. Bluemound Rd. P.O. Box 13819 Milwaukee, WI 53213

Prices, contents and availability subject to change without notice.

1112

1112